THE WIFE
PROLOGUE

The Shrew. From a misericord in the church
of St Lawrence, Ludlow

THE
WIFE OF BATH'S
PROLOGUE & TALE

FROM THE CANTERBURY TALES

BY

GEOFFREY CHAUCER

Edited with Introduction, Notes and Glossary by

JAMES WINNY

Revised by

SEAN KANE *and* BEVERLEY WINNY

CAMBRIDGE
UNIVERSITY PRESS

PUBLISHED BY THE PRESS SYNDICATE OF THE UNIVERSITY OF CAMBRIDGE
The Pitt Building, Trumpington Street, Cambridge, United Kingdom

CAMBRIDGE UNIVERSITY PRESS
The Edinburgh Building, Cambridge CB2 2RU, UK   http://www.cup.cam.ac.uk
40 West 20th Street, New York, NY 10011–4211, USA   http://www.cup.org
10 Stamford Road, Oakleigh, Melbourne 3166, Australia

First published 1965
Twenty-third printing 1993
Revised edition 1994
Ninth printing 1999

Printed in the United Kingdom at the University Press, Cambridge

A catalogue record for this book is available from the British Library

Library of Congress Cataloguing in Publication data
Chaucer, Geoffrey, d. 1400.
[Wife of Bath's tale]
The wife of Bath's prologue & tale from the Canterbury tales / by
Geoffrey Chaucer.—Rev. ed. / James Winny.
p.   cm.—(Selected tales from Chaucer
Includes bibliographical references.
1. Christian pilgrims and pilgrimages—England—Canterbury—
—Poetry.   I. Winny, James. II. Title. III. Title: Wife of
Bath's prologue and tale from the Canterbury tales. IV. Series.
PR1868.W59   1994
821′.1–dc20   93–33751   CIP

ISBN 0 521 46689 X

The cover illustration shows a manuscript illumination depicting
Geoffrey Chaucer, reproduced by permission of The Huntingdon
Library, San Marino, California

CONTENTS

It lives in gusto, be it foul or fair, high or low, rich or poor, mean or elevated—It has as much delight in conceiving an Iago as an Imogen. What shocks the virtuous philosopher, delights the chameleon poet. It does no harm from its relish of the dark side of things any more than from its taste for the bright one; because they both end in speculation.

KEATS, *Letter to Richard Woodhouse*

FOR EILEEN AND HUGH

INTRODUCTION

With the challenge of her opening word, 'experience', the Wife of Bath bursts upon the pilgrimage with the unexpectedness of a bomb, to introduce herself and a group of three connected tales. She begins unannounced, an emphatic voice proclaiming a long familiarity with the miseries of married life, and dismissing the hearsay opinions of authority with the assurance of her own expert knowledge. She needs no formal introduction. Before she reaches her admission of having married five husbands at church door—an achievement previously mentioned in *The General Prologue*—her audacity and forthrightness have already identified her. The pent-up energy and physical stamina implicit in Chaucer's account of her many pilgrimages, and reflected in her startling costume, have taken fire before the Host can call her forward. Without waiting to be invited, the Wife has launched herself upon the shameless autobiographical confession which holds the pilgrims fascinated, and with one exception speechless, to the end.

This seemingly inexhaustible private story, only a few lines shorter than the introductory prologue to the whole collection of tales, serves two important purposes. Most obviously, it gives the dimension of living actuality to a character seen previously only as a striking figure in a group photograph: as sharp-edged and brilliant as a manuscript illumination, but unheard and motionless. The portrait of the Wife in *The General Prologue*, with gaudy stockings and outsized hat, an incongruous obsession with husbands and pilgrimages, and the partial

deafness that Chaucer leaves for the moment unex-
plained, is both a finished sketch of character and a
tantalizing promise—a source of future disclosures
which the poet postpones, as if too reticent to continue.
Now, in her prologue, the Wife is able to speak for
herself. Unlike the narrator of *The General Prologue*,
she withholds nothing, but takes the pilgrims into her
confidence with an unblushing frankness that scorns
half-measures. Her confessions do much more than fill
in the details of the Wife's private history which
Chaucer had hinted at earlier. They allow Chaucer to
range across a wide tract of common human experience,
and to represent the feel of its vigorous, rough-grained
reality through contact with the Wife's energy and
liveliness.

As the Wife's introduction to her tale grows into an
extended autobiography, Chaucer admits the extraord-
inary length of her preamble through the Friar, who
voices (line 829) the surprise which her audience must
feel. Most of the prologues to the pilgrims' tales run to a
length of between thirty and eighty lines, and only the
Pardoner—a professional public speaker—takes over a
hundred lines to introduce himself. Chaucer's reasons
for overloading the Wife's Prologue in this way have to
be understood within the imaginative design of *The
Canterbury Tales*. This composite work is not simply a
collection of stories paired off with their individual
tellers, but a poem whose interests are divided between
story-telling and a satirical analysis of human personality, exploiting the unlimited resources of both. These
two basic subjects of *The Canterbury Tales* are brought
together by Chaucer's association of particular personal-

ity with literary type in the tales, and in the varied reception—hilarious, scornfully impatient, sentimentally moved—which the pilgrims give to the stories. The lively human intertext of the actual tales, supplied by the conversational links between them, shows that Chaucer was attempting to achieve something more complex than a connected series of fabliaux, courtly romances and moral exempla. By presenting his tales as spoken stories coloured by each speaker's personality, and by reproducing the rhythms and vocabulary of colloquial English at the expense of the more literary language he had favoured hitherto, Chaucer gave his final work a living immediacy. When we recognize the particular creative task that Chaucer was undertaking, we understand why the Wife of Bath ran away with him. Although nominally her Prologue is subordinate to the much shorter Tale which it precedes, it is in the long preamble of marital gossip and reminiscence that Chaucer captures the tumbling freshness and vitality of popular speech at first hand:

> What eyleth yow to grucche thus and grone?
> Is it for ye wolde have my queynte allone?
> Wy, taak it al! lo, have it every deel!
> Peter! I shrewe yow, but ye love it weel.   (443–6)

Even when the Wife at last begins her Tale, the temptation to lapse into the more exuberant style of her personal story for another twenty lines proves irresistible. It looks as though Chaucer did not willingly revert to the quieter idiom of the narrative proper, where the Wife's personality must be subordinated to the needs of the Tale.

By suggesting that the private affairs of a middle-aged woman could provide the subject of a long narrative poem, Chaucer gave his audience a second surprise. In general, medieval literature makes use of low-life characters in much the same way as Shakespeare does, to embody laughable or disreputable aspects of human nature. The more serious human concerns are usually treated through knights and gentlefolk, such as appear in Chaucer's courtly tales. When the ordinary people are admitted—artisans, tradespeople, peasants and servants —they usually perform a limited function, often farcical. The unfortunate carpenter of *The Miller's Tale* is an example. Chaucer does not attempt to make a convincing individual of him, but gives him only such characteristics—credulity, fearfulness, infatuation with his attractive young wife—as needed to bring about his comic downfall. The serious function of low-life characters in medieval fiction is confined to the moral and satirical works where they embody vices and other forms of corruption, though here too they are depicted as grotesquely comic. In *Piers Plowman*, for instance, Avarice is personified as a dishonest innkeeper who confesses how he and his wife have increased their profits by adulterating their beer and giving short measure:

> Peny ale and poding ale she poured togidres
> For laboreres and for low folke; that lay by himselve.
> The best ale lay in my boure, or in my bedchambre,
> And whoso bommed therof boughte it therafter
> A galoun for a grote, God wote, no lesse;
> And yet it cam in cupmel: this craft my wyf used.[1]

4

As this passage suggests, a character who embarked upon a confession of personal habits was likely to be displaying—necessarily without reserve—the nature of some particular form of corruption, whether social or individual. A similar kind of self-incriminating confession was sometimes put into the mouths of bad characters in medieval drama. In its full maturity this tradition was to produce the comic soliloquies in which Falstaff describes his immorality and cowardice with as much impudent unconcern as the Wife reveals her technique of cheating and outwitting husbands.

At first glance—a comically outsize figure from common life, embodying the vices of rage, cupidity and lust, and boasting of her outrageous exploits—the Wife of Bath might seem to fall squarely within this satirical tradition. But she is also, in the amplest sense of the word, a character. Her indiscretions and shortcomings do not stand as types of moral weakness, but as details of a complicated personality. The impression of living presence which Chaucer creates through the movement and linguistic colour of the Wife's narrative extends well beyond the simple basis of moral category or literary type upon which he has built. Other material drawn into her boisterous individuality, whether from folklore or from such accredited literary sources as the *Roman de la Rose* and the writings of St Jerome, make her one of the most completely realized of the portraits.

Some hints of the audacious character which the Wife herself is to lay bare appear in the thumbnail portrait of

---

[1] *Piers Plowman*, B-text, V, 220-5. *Poding ale*, 'cheap ale'; *bommed*, 'tasted'; *cupmel*, 'cupfuls'.

The General Prologue. Chaucer notes her faulty hearing and her widely spaced teeth, though without suggesting that this feature becomes the Wife, as she will claim in her Prologue. He mentions the florid complexion, 'boold . . . and fair, and reed of hewe' (*General Prologue*, 460), which insinuates itself through the Wife's energetic manner of speaking. The poet's many references to her dress—coverchief, stockings, shoes, wimple, hat and foot-mantle, variously approved as fine, rich, new and conspicuous—prepare us for the Wife's allusion to her wardrobe of 'gaye scarlet gites', which moths had no opportunity of spoiling. Not all the points of this introductory portrait are taken up in *The Wife's Prologue*. The passion for sight-seeing and adventure which has driven her three times to Jerusalem is barely mentioned again—her fourth husband died conveniently when she came home from one of these pilgrimages—and while Chaucer remarks that she 'koude muchel of wandringe by the weye' (*General Prologue*, 469), nothing more is heard of this promising topic. But when so much is given, it would be absurd to cavil over such omissions. *The Wife's Prologue* does not attempt simply to enlarge the earlier description of her character, but takes some of its features as the starting-point of a biographical self-portrait. The Wife describes the moments of her past life which delight her most to remember, rather than the details of her appearance which an observer would find most striking. In her prologue the Wife presents her own view of herself.

On the other occasions when Chaucer allows his pilgrims to speak for themselves, his intentions are ironic. The Monk, and later the Friar, contributes to his own portrait in *The General Prologue* by justifying his unorthodox behaviour in a short argument that Chaucer reproduces without comment. Neither speaker recognizes that he is condemning himself out of his own mouth. Why should he drive himself crazy with studying, the Monk demands,

> Or swinken with his handes, and laboure,
> As Austin bit? How shal the world be served?
> (*General Prologue*, 186–7)

The argument seems reasonable only to those who forget that monastic life was intended to protect a religious community from the distractions of the world which the Monk is so anxious to serve. When he protests that the cloistered life prevents his taking a hand in worldly affairs, the Monk is attacking the whole purpose of his religious vocation. The Friar betrays himself just as unwittingly. For a man of his social dignity to be seen in the company of the poor and the outcast, he declares, would be entirely unfitting:

> It is nat honest, it may nat avaunce,
> For to deelen with no swich poraille.
> (*General Prologue*, 246–7)

He means to be impressive, but displays only self-importance and inhumanity. Chaucer quotes both speakers as though respectfully, aware that in fact their arguments reveal the true character of each pilgrim behind an outwardly convincing argument. We might expect to find the same ironic technique applied to the Wife's long account of herself.

Though evident, it is applied subtly in her case. Her lack of reticence about her marital affairs, and her

7

outspokenness on the subjects of second marriages and
the sexual obligations of husbands, typify her attitude
throughout the Prologue. Unlike any other member of
the company, she apparently entertains no illusions
about her own nature, and is too much amused by her
own moral lapses to wish to hide them. Her warning to
the pilgrims of disclosures in store follows a clear
announcement that the Wife has long since come to
terms with the impulses which govern her. 'He spak to
hem that wolde live parfitly', she remarks of Christ's
doctrine,

> And lordinges, by youre leve, that am nat I.   (112)

What she is, evolves from the clash of astrological forces
that has produced her incongruously divided character.
The weakness which draws her to an attractive lover,
and the marks of martial temperament which give her
face its unfeminine boldness, are admitted with the same
unabashed frankness. The influence of Venus, she
acknowledges openly,

> made me I koude noght withdrawe
> My chambre of Venus from a good felawe.
> Yet have I Martes mark upon my face.   (617–19)

She observes the working of her sexual instincts with an
interest both absorbed and critically detached, setting
her own emotional vagaries in the larger context of her
sense of womanly nature, which she describes with
familiar understanding. 'We wommen han', she remarks
pleasantly,

> In this matere a queynte fantasie;
> Waite what thing we may nat lightly have,

> Therafter wol we crie al day and crave.
> Forbede us thing, and that desiren we.   (516–19)

She makes public the most intimate details of her married life with the same cheerful abandon, acknowledging the sexual frustration that prompted her to torment her old and half-impotent husbands, as though it were merely an amusing sidelight on feminine psychology. Her pointblank references to the body and to sexual activity are part of the Wife's refusal to temporize.

Where her behaviour involves ironies, the Wife is often their most appreciative critic. Her reminiscences could be read as a comic satire on women and married life in which the speaker unconsciously proves the truth of the antifeminist argument at the same time as she tries to discredit her opponents' case. A good deal of the Prologue is taken up with an account of the way the Wife made life unbearable for her old husbands by just such rebellious and self-assertive behaviour as the spokesmen of the early Church had condemned. Taken in isolation, this long passage (235–378) might suggest that the Wife is betraying herself in the same unwitting manner as the Monk and the Friar. When she tells the pilgrims how she ridiculed her husband's perpetual grumbling, the Wife appears not to notice that her account of their married life completely justifies his grievances:

> Thou liknest eek wommenes love to helle,
> To bareyne lond, ther water may nat dwelle.
> Thou liknest it also to wilde fyr;
> The moore it brenneth, the moore it hath desir
> To consume every thing that brent wole be.

> Thou seyest, right as wormes shende a tree,
> Right so a wyf destroyeth hire housbonde.   (371–7)

The irony of the situation lies in the Wife's repeating a rightful complaint as evidence of the exasperations which she has to bear. The comparison with wild fire applies aptly to a woman who has consumed five husbands, but the congruity appears to pass over the Wife's head. Like the Monk, she seems unconscious of betraying herself through her own self-justification. 'Thow seist we wives wol oure vices hide', she continues, still repeating her retort to her husband's rebuke,

> Til we be fast, and thanne we wol hem shewe—
> Wel may that be a proverbe of a shrewe!   (283–4)

But the Wife has already admitted to treating her old husbands in just this calculating fashion. 'They had me yeven hir lond and hir tresoor', she explains cheerfully,

> Me neded nat do lenger diligence
> To winne hir love, or doon hem reverence . . .
>   (205–6)

> What sholde I taken keep hem for to plese,
> But it were for my profit and myn ese?   (213–14)

Both in form and in tone her question recalls the Monk's argument; but Chaucer gives the irony a further twist. The Wife seems entirely aware of the contradictions of her attitude, and shares the joke of her quick-witted duplicity with the pilgrims by describing her technique of gaining 'maistrie' over a nonplussed husband. To invalidate his accusation she brings his own charge against him before he can begin, and turns his catalogue of grievances back upon him as proof of his peevish and fretful mind. These inconsistencies of behaviour are not merely recognized by the Wife but deliberately designed, and related to her audience with mocking relish. To ensnare the attractive Jankin she employs different tactics, but again with an apparent critical self-awareness that allows her to appreciate the comedy of her shameless deception. 'I bar hym on honde he hadde enchanted me' (575), she tells the pilgrims; and after explaining how she pretended to have dreamt that Jankin was trying to murder her in her bed, she mimics the coy suggestion which brought him into the net:

> But yet I hope that he shal do me good.   (580)

So far from being an unconscious victim of irony, the Wife appears to be its master and exponent. Like Chaucer himself, she possesses the power of critical perception that gives a narrative its cutting edge, and proves the comprehensive awareness of the teller.

The Wife knows herself to be more than a match for any man, whatever the field of contest. The task of winning and retaining the 'maistrie' presents no problems to a woman who can outwit her husbands so adroitly, arguing that since man is woman's intellectual superior, he should see the need to give way to her whims:

> Oon of us two moste bowen, doutelees;
> And sith a man is moore resonable
> Than womman is, ye moste been suffrable.   (440–2)

The Wife's fourth husband, however, presents a more serious challenge to her moral supremacy. Electing to find his satisfaction outside marriage, perhaps with a more docile partner, he disables the sexual magnetism which gives the Wife her ultimate hold over men. To this affront she can reply only with the crudest of weapons, and at the end boast of no better success than being quits with her tormentor. Her fifth venture, the outcome of a love-match with a young man half her age, begins with an impulsive abandoning of authority and possessions to the husband—a mistake retrieved only after the convulsive effort that leaves the Wife permanently deaf in one ear.

By regaining the upper hand after this lapse of judgement, the Wife reaffirms the principle upon which she bases her conception of marriage. It is an unending war of the sexes in which the Wife has no intention of accepting the subordinate position. She will be satisfied only with 'maistrie', and the unconditional surrender of her partner. When she reveals her divided temperament,

> Myn ascendent was Taur, and Mars therinne,   (613)

the Wife gives fair warning of the warlike disposition underlying her general affability. However clamorous her desire for personal pleasure, her driving impulse to dominate will not be content with the secondary satisfaction of fine clothes, amusing entertainment, and all that is implied by the term 'daliaunce'. Love of 'maistrie' determines the form of the sexual relationship as it does her general management of marital affairs. 'An housbonde I wol have', she declares roundly,

> Which shal be bothe my dettour and my thral . . .
> (155)

> I have the power duringe al my lyf
> Upon his propre body, and noght he.   (158–9)

Introduction

To see the Wife simply as the exponent of an arch-feminist view of womanly sovereignty in marriage, later to be contested by the Franklin and the Clerk, is to accept an unadventurously literal reading of a richly ironic work. The attack on 'auctoritee' which opens her Prologue shows her challenging a more formidable opponent than a mere husband. Ostensibly confronting the scholarly authority of the Church Fathers from the standpoint of common experience, she meets them on their own ground of learned disputation and contests their reading of Scripture. If the Church denies moral sanction to second marriages, how does it explain Christ's references to the five husbands of the Samaritan woman? Abraham, Jacob and Solomon are all accounted wise holy men, yet all were married many times without incurring any stigma. Where does God expressly forbid marrying, or enjoin us to remain chaste? Did not even St Paul refuse to go so far as this, merely advising those to remain single who could live happily unmarried? Virginity may be morally superior to the married state, but was not the choice left open to the individual without reproach? In the face of this argument, the educated reader of Chaucer's time might wonder what use is being made of scriptural authority by a woman who is 'somdel deef' (*General Prologue*, 448; see Mark 4:23), and who claims analogy with another woman by a well who had five husbands and was rebuked by Christ (John 4:6ff.). 'What that he mente therby, I kan nat seyn' (20), says the Wife, oblivious to the import of the passage, just as she conveniently forgets the account of Solomon's lust in old age which made him turn away from the Lord and follow strange gods (1 Kings 11).

After this dislocation of Scripture, the Wife turns from textual exegesis to the argument of commonsense and everyday experience, where she is naturally at home. If marriage is displeasing to God and better avoided, what are the sexual organs for? 'Trusteth right wel', she assures her audience, 'they were nat maad for noght' (118). She hardly needs to point out the absurdity of arguing that 'oure bothe thinges smale' (121) were intended to serve purely practical ends, by distinguishing male from female and by acting as waste-pipes. Experience, the touchstone of the Wife's realistic wisdom, 'woot wel it is noght so' (124). Their simple functions are obvious to everyone; but in addition, the Wife asserts, the reproductive organs are designed to provide particular physical sensations—'ese of engendrure' (127–8)—which may be enjoyed as a completely legitimate form of pleasure. This does not mean, she concedes, that everyone who feels inclined must put their equipment to use indiscriminately; but if there is a proper place in the scheme of things for virginity, so is there for those who feel themselves called to the more strenuous occupation of wifehood. 'In swich estaat as God hath cleped us', she announces cheerfully,

> I wol persevere; I nam nat precius.
> In wyfhod I wol use myn instrument
> As frely as my Makere hath it sent.
> If I be daungerous, God yeve me sorwe!¹ (148–51)

Through this appeal to common experience—'say ye no?' (123)—the Wife presents a case for the kind of sexual freedom that she has chosen instinctively

---

¹ *Precius*, 'fastidious'; *daungerous*, 'reluctant'.

throughout her life. In developing her argument, from its initial references to Holy Writ, through the sudden shift of ground to sexual anatomy, to her demonstration that the activities of wifehood are her appointed calling, the Wife shows a degree of mental ingenuity matching that of her physical resilience. Adopting the method of Scholastic argument, she has contested the prohibitive morality of the medieval Church and planted her own pragmatic doctrine on the ruins.

The Wife seems to be declaring hostility to the moral outlook which could impugn the whole function of woman within marriage. The medieval church spokesman, believing woman responsible for the Fall and its accompanying disasters, and committed to a celibate existence, were not all capable of discussing the nature of woman objectively. Regarding sexual instinct as a source of degrading weakness, the Church found it easy to see woman as the temptress whose attractions led man to sin, and to repeat St Paul's opinion that it was better to avoid contamination by remaining unmarried. The common-sense objection voiced by the Wife, that without loss of virginity the world could not be peopled, had been answered by St Jerome: 'Marriage replenishes the earth; virginity fills heaven.' If the moral caution against marriage was not a sufficient deterrent, there remained St Paul's realistic warning about 'the trouble in the flesh' (1 Corinthians 7:28), a topic which the Wife is well fitted to speak about and refers to as marital 'woe'. The Church's attitude towards life becomes the target of her ridicule as she declares rebelliously that she will use her womanly instrument as generously as her Maker intended. Yet in the 850 lines in which the Wife talks about herself almost without drawing breath, the silences in the text speak the loudest. Why do children go unmentioned? Why does she not tell what happened to the fifth husband? Where does the Church say, 'Allas, allas, that evere love was sinne' (614)?

The opening phase of *The Wife's Prologue* presents the speaker as the representative of experience, challenging a well-established opponent to a contest of philosophical 'maistrie'. Against the accumulated learning of her times she poses the pungent wisdom of proverbial sayings, and the certainties of knowledge which she has gained in the cut and thrust of daily events. One side of the contest fetches its opinions from written commentaries, not consulting the evidence of tangible fact but regarding the pronouncements of the Church and the Schoolmen as unassailable authority. The other bases itself upon the certainty of everyday events, and the pressing realities of human affairs, where learned opinions seem insubstantial. Rejecting authority outright, when she is not bending it to her uses, the Wife declares her faith in a woman's intuitive judgement, and bases herself squarely upon the truth and reliability of general experience.

From this we might suppose that Chaucer sided with intuition and experience against the arid, inflexible forms of medieval learning. But here we must move cautiously. There are gaps and silences in the Wife's reasoning from experience, just as there are in the Church's reasoning from authority. Where is Chaucer's allegiance here? His poetry contains impressive proof of his wide-ranging intellectual interests and of his close familiarity with works of philosophy and literature in at least three

European languages beside his own. His translation of Boethius and his scientific treatise on the astrolabe reveal the scholarly mind which kept company with Chaucer's creative imagination, often showing its presence by injecting half-comic allusions to learned topics into the poems. *The Nun's Priest's Tale* is incongruously spiced with references to predestination, mermaids, dream-lore, classical authors and the practice of rhetoric, which can be put down to Sir John's studious turn of mind. *The Franklin's Tale* includes some abstruse astrological calculations, conveniently fathered upon the 'subtil clerk' to whom Aurelius appeals for help. This feature of Chaucer's poetry had shown itself much earlier. The Eagle who carries off the poet in *The House of Fame* reads him a lecture on Aristotelian dynamics, offers to instruct him in astronomy, points out the 'ayerissh bestes' described by Plato, and congratulates himself upon having explained things clearly without 'figures of poetrie, or colours of rethorike'. Here too the display of learning is used as a half-comic device. *The Wife's Prologue* contains a still more astonishing parade of erudition. The close references to Holy Writ might be expected of so regular a churchgoer, though the Wife must have been unusually attentive during readings from the Epistle to the Corinthians. It is the acquaintance with Patristic and classical authors that seems so remark-able in the Wife. Her biblical knowledge has been supplemented by a detailed study of St Jerome's treatise against Jovinian, with its long extract from Theophras-tus's account of the miseries of married life. She seems to have some knowledge of Tertullian, and to be acquain-ted with the long rhetorical work compiled by Valerius

Maximus. She refers to the *Ars Amatoria* and the *Metamorphoses* of Ovid, and shows her familiarity with classical legend by speaking of Clytemnestra, Eriphyle, Pasiphaë and Livilla. She knows Boethius and Dante, and is able to quote from Seneca and Juvenal. She mentions Ptolemy's *Almageste* twice, and suggests by alluding to the tomb of Darius that she had explored some of the by-ways of medieval literature. The *Alexandreid* of de Chatillon cannot have been in great demand with fourteenth-century readers.

So much learning would have been unaccountable in the Wife had she not taken a scholar of Oxford as her fifth husband. In point of character Jankin is much inferior to his counterpart on the pilgrimage. He takes advantage of his position in the household to flirt with the Wife, and helps her to outwit her fourth husband, promising to marry her as soon as she is widowed. Jankin keeps his word, but rapidly changes into a spiteful misogynist who concentrates all his learning upon the task of humiliating the Wife. It is from his hateful compilation of antifeminist works that she learns of the great churchman

> that highte Seint Jerome,
> That made a book again Jovinian;   (674–5)

and of Valerius and Theophrastus, who supported his outrageous opinion of married women, though Jankin's scholarship does not account for the Wife's ability to quote from Dante in her Tale. It hardly needs saying that this erudition is neither hers nor Jankin's, but Chaucer's. The introduction of a scholar-husband enables the poet to express some of his own intellectual interests through the Wife's mouth without straining probability too far. An element of comic incongruity is present, but a serious purpose is also involved. However closely the world of tangible fact and sensation absorbs him, Chaucer has allegiance to the outlook and opinions of writers who dominated the world of medieval thought. As a poet, he has a peculiarly intense awareness of the qualities of material objects. It is characteristic of him to notice that the Wife's stocking, 'of fyn scarlet reed', are

Ful streite yteyd, and shoes ful moiste and newe;
(*General Prologue*, 459)

picking up telling details of costume with a shrewd eye. It is this same sharpness of perception which he shares with the Wife as she follows her husband's coffin, by making her suddenly conscious of Jankin's trim and attractive legs. The world of natural creation, with its unlimited diversity of forms, obviously excited Chaucer deeply; but his reading provided an alternative field of experience in which he immersed himself with similar eagerness. His imaginative awareness of the physical objects that he described with such insight was counter-balanced by the scholarly interests developed by his wide reading, which made him part of the intellectual consciousness of medieval Europe. *The Wife's Prologue* brings into conflict forces that represent contradictory impulses within Chaucer, one drawing its stimulus from the impact of physical experience upon his senses, the other from the excitement of scholarship and ideas. This conflict, implicit in the Wife's attack upon an authority seeking to discredit the realities which she embodies, comes to a head when she marries a bookish husband whose conception of woman has been formed by his academic studies.

Despite its sense of immediate contact with the solid realities of existence, *The Wife's Prologue* does not entirely support a view of Chaucer as a writer who values life experience over cultural authority. Although she indignantly disputes the Patristic judgement of married women, the Wife is herself a conspicuous example of all the wifely vices traditionally imputed to her sex. In fact, the outline of the Wife's character comes in very large part from the very authorities whom she attacks. In particular, whole passages of the *Epistola adversus Jovinianum* have been drafted into the Wife's protest against the vexations that she has to suffer from her husbands. 'Horses, asses, cattle', St Jerome had written, quoting a work of Theophrastus now lost, 'even slaves of the smallest worth, clothes, kettles, wooden seats, cups and earthenware pitchers, are first tried and then bought: a wife is the only thing that is not shown before she is married, for fear she may not give satisfaction.' Taken over by the Wife, the sense of Theophrastus's complaint is ironically reversed upon him. The Wife repeats the accusation as an example of the indignities put upon her by an old and peevish husband, and by so doing is able to use the original complaint as proof of its author's obstinate folly:

> Thou seist that oxen, asses, hors, and houndes,
> They been assayed at diverse stoundes;
> Bacins, lavours, er that men hem bye,
> Spoones and stooles, and al swich housbondrie,
> And so been pottes, clothes, and array;
> But folk of wives maken noon assay,

Til they be wedded; olde dotard shrewe!
And thanne, seistow, we wol oure vices shewe.

(285–92)

The irony of allowing the Wife to quote St Jerome against himself provides a scholarly joke that Chaucer keeps discreetly hidden, though allowing his readers to enjoy the more obvious point that the husband has good reason for his complaint. Theophrastus may have been right, after all.

The close parallel between the Wife's vigorously argued view and the attitude of St Jerome is expected.[1] The vernacular energy of the Wife's attack on her husband suggests that Chaucer is reproducing popular ideas on marriage, where in fact all she says is modelled upon part of a fourth-century treatise—an 'auctoritee'—written by one of the most influential of early Christian scholars. Jerome's ideas are invigorated by the homely form into which Chaucer renders his Latin, but they remain easily recognizable in their new guise. Chaucer has devised a means of combining his disparate interests in a happy marriage of erudition and direct transcription from life. The passage represents an imaginative synthesis, reconciling the cultural authority and life experience that underlies Chaucer's poetry. This synthesis has the directness of a speaking voice and the colloquial liveliness of gossip, but neither of these important qualities is obtained by abandoning the element of bookishness which had informed Chaucer's earlier poetry. However well concealed, the poet's learning exerts its pressures upon his work.

[1] See Appendix 2, pp. 122–4, where twelve such parallels are noted.

Introduction

The marriage of learning and experience is less happily effected in *The Wife's Tale*. For reasons discussed elsewhere,[1] Chaucer's matching of tale to teller could not always be very exact; and not many of the pilgrims become more fully realized characters as a result of their stories. In some earlier arrangement of *The Canterbury Tales* Chaucer appears to have given the Wife the tale which later was assigned to the Shipman: a fabliau turning upon a woman's deception of her merchant husband, which would appeal to the Wife's pride in her outwitting of jealously watchful old men. The romance of the Loathly Lady, which was then substituted for this fabliau, suits the Wife better in respect of its concern with sovereignty in marriage, but in other respects seems alien to the character which her Prologue reveals in such detail. Her choice of a fairy-tale is at best improbable. It might be argued that Chaucer is hinting at a pattern of romance wish-fulfilment hidden beneath the Wife's raucous exterior, but where she brims over into her Tale with characteristic boldness of language, asserting that the notion of woman's constancy 'is nat worth a rake-stele' (949), both her tone and her frankness discredit the suggestion. The more restrained idiom of the Tale proper, on the other hand, suggests that a courtly narrator has replaced the Wife. It cannot be she who makes the wry comment on the celebrations at the Knight's marriage to his loathly bride:

> Now wolden som men seye, paraventure,
> That for my necligence I do no cure
> To tellen yow the joye and al th'array

[1] See the introduction to *The General Prologue* (Cambridge, 1965), pp. 8–10.

That at the feeste was that ilke day.
To which thing shortly answeren I shal:
I seye ther nas no joye ne feeste at al.   (1073–8)

This rhetorical joke, where the narrator, as a red herring, accuses himself of oversight, before disclosing that there was no feast, is entirely Chaucer's own comic manner, and far removed from the Wife's ribald sense of fun. Vernacular energy gives way to an urbanely humorous tone impossible to associate with the Wife. Chaucer is failing to maintain the creative synthesis achieved—and, as it seems, dramatically represented—in *The Wife's Prologue*.

This failure is most apparent in the discussion which occupies a quarter of *The Wife's Tale*. It might be conceded that the Wife could tell a fairy-tale, but not that she should become involved in a serious philosophical debate on the nature of 'gentillesse'. The woman who becomes enraged when another wife precedes her during the offertory, who cheats and deludes her husbands, seizing their wealth by force of 'maistrie' and even exacting payment for their use of her body, shows not the remotest interest in the ideal of gentle behaviour which forms the hub of her Tale. The exhortation, 'Reedeth Senek, and redeth eek Boece' (1168), is just as improbable, whether the Wife or an independent Loathly Lady is supposed to be speaking. Chaucer has been unable to reconcile his philosophical interests with the individuality of the storyteller, and has chosen to accept inconsistency of character in order to develop his scholarly theme.

Without the discussion of gentillesse the Tale would have been disproportionately short, but altogether more

plausible as the Wife's contribution to the general
entertainment. Although a figure of folklore, the
Loathly Lady shares some important features with the
Wife. She is usually described as terrifyingly ugly,
rapacious and tyrannical, refusing to accept any frustration of her will and presenting a deadly menace to
every man whom she confronts. Only when she finds a
man ready to carry out all her wishes courteously and
without protest is she softened, and a sudden transformation changes her from an ugly hag into a beautiful and
companionable wife. From the account of her behaviour
given in her Prologue, the Wife of Bath seems in many
respects a human counterpart of this supernatural figure,
having something of the same forbidding appearance,
much the same insatiable appetite, and a tyrannical will
to match the Lady's. To complete the parallel, when her
demands have been satisfied she is prepared to become a
faithful and loving wife. After the battle which brought
Jankin to his knees, the Wife assures the pilgrims,

> I was to him as kinde
> As any wyf from Denmark unto Inde,
> And also trewe, and so was he to me.   (823–5)

Chaucer's decision to allot this tale to the Wife may have
been prompted by the general similarity between her
character and the nature of the Loathly Lady in the
folk-stories of his age. In some versions of the story, as
for example the ballad *King Henry*,[1] the magic transformation of the Lady is not prompted by any choices she

---

[1] Included in the *Oxford Book of Ballads* (1989), pp. 64–7. For a
complete survey of this folklore theme in early literature, see Sigmund
Eisner, *A Tale of Wonder* (Wexford, 1957).

offers, but follows a succession of courteous acts by the hero as a reward for his dutiful service. This traditional form of the Tale brought into view a problem which had occupied several medieval writers, and which appealed strongly to Chaucer's interest in moral and philosophical issues. The question of what constitutes nobility or gentillesse had been debated by Dante a century earlier in his *Convivio*, and treated less intensively by the earlier writers mentioned in *The Wife's Tale*. Part of the *Roman de la Rose* translated by Chaucer deals with the same subject, Love declaring that he intends

> To clepe no wight in noo ages
> Oonly gentil for his linages,
> But whoso is vertuous.

Chaucer had given a clear sign of his personal interest in the *Ballade of Gentillesse*, which surveys the subject in his own way and draws the same conclusions as Dante and the other authors whom he had studied. The homily addressed to the Knight in *The Wife's Tale* represents Chaucer's fullest discussion of the issues involved. Like his ballade, the Lady's argument contains nothing original in the way of ideas and outlook. It allows Chaucer to express his personal response to ideas which had become part of a tradition of European thought, by repeating an established argument in more homely terms as part of a moral tale for English audiences. With the introduction of this subject the folk-story drops into the background, superseded by Chaucer's greater interest in the moral question which has developed out of a make-believe situation. At the same time the narrative tone becomes quieter and more dignified, exchanging the vigorous popular idiom which supplies part of the Wife's character for the cultured restraint of a courtly poet addressing an audience of gentlefolk:

> And he that wole han pris of his gentrie,
> For he was boren of a gentil hous,
> And hadde his eldres noble and vertuous,
> And nel himselven do no gentil dedis,
> Ne folwen his gentil auncestre that deed is,
> He nis nat gentil, be he duc or erl.   (1152–7)

Here Chaucer is no longer attempting to reproduce the sensation of living experience. He is writing as a poet mindful of the civilizing traditions underlying European literature, and helping to consolidate the standards from which his own poetry draws example and impetus. This aspect of Chaucer, less immediately arresting than the comic vitality of *The Wife's Prologue*, acts as a counterpoise in the creative resolution of his final work. The alert awareness of material qualities which seizes upon the moist feel of new leather or the sharpness of a pilgrim's spurs is balanced by a critical scrutiny, whose judgements are backed by a wide acquaintance with fourteenth-century thought and its written sources. The outcome, in Chaucer's finest poetry, represents a merging of intellectual urbanity with an instinctive feeling for the material identity of things, where each form of awareness complements and strengthens the other.

SOME NOTES ON CHAUCER'S
USAGE OF MIDDLE ENGLISH

'KAN', 'KNOWEN' AND 'WITEN'

In modern English the same verb is used to denote two different kinds of knowing: those represented in French by *savoir* and *connaître*, and in German by *können* and *wissen*. Middle English allowed the same distinction to be made between practical ability, or know-how, and intellectual grasp. *Kan* and *koude* convey the sense of knowing how to do something, or of possessing special talent or expertise. The modern forms 'can' and 'could' are not a satisfactory equivalent for these strong Middle English verbs. Thus,

if that she kan her good	if she knows what's to her advantage
I koude noght withdrawe	I didn't know how to deny
wel kan Dant speken	well does Dante know how to express this; or, Dante puts this admirably

Knowen is used to denote various kinds of intellectual apprehension—distinguishing, recognizing, learning, detecting, and so on. As a rule, this verb is not to be translated simply as 'to know'. Thus,

to knowe a female from a male	to distinguish women from men
this knowen lecchours by experiençe	lechers discover this from experience
he knew of mo proverbes	he was acquainted with, or, had learnt, more proverbs

27

The very irregular verb *witen*, meaning 'to have knowledge of', or 'to know as a fact', is used where the simple sense 'to know' is required. Thus,

no wight that wiste	no one who knew
Wostow why?	do you know why?
every wight woot this	everyone knows this

But note an unusual case at line 124, *experience woot wel*, 'experience proves clearly'.

'WOL', 'MAY' AND 'MOOT'

The strong verb *wol* or *wil* serves two different purposes. Used as a main verb it means 'to desire' or 'to wish for', but as an auxiliary it generally corresponds to modern 'will'. Thus,

I wol him noght	I do not want him at all
a thing that no man wole	something nobody wants
we wol been holden wise	we like to be thought wise

On the other hand, the statement, *An housbonde I wol have, I wol nat lette*, expresses determined purpose rather than desire. In many cases the two senses of *wol* merge together, and the degree to which desire is implied must be judged from the context. For example:

thou woldest loke me in thy chiste	you would, if you could, lock me up with your valuables + you would like to lock me up
I wolde nat of him corrected be	I refused to let him correct me + I hated him to correct me

To convey the sense expressed by 'can' in modern English, Chaucer sometimes uses *kan*; as in the line, *Now kan no man see none elves mo.* More commonly he uses *may*, and *mighte* for modern 'could'. The following examples show that the sense of the verb is not conditional, as in modern English:

with empty hand men may none haukes lure	one cannot attract hawks without a lure
whan he is oold, and may noght do	when he is old, and cannot perform
ther may no man devise	no one can imagine

When Chaucer requires the permissive sense of modern English 'may', he uses *moot*, as in the common expression *so moot I thee*, 'so may I prosper'. This verb sometimes hardens into a sense corresponding to modern 'must': in *yet out it moot*, 'but it must come out', and *as wives mooten*, 'as wives are obliged to'.

'BUT'

But is used in three distinct constructions in the present work. They are:

(i) With the sense of 'merely' or 'only': as at line 13, *but ones*, 'only once'; line 881, *doon hem but dishonour*, 'merely bring them into disgrace'.

(ii) Meaning 'except' or 'unless'. For example: line 438, *but ye do*, 'unless you do'; line 1066, *but if thy wyf I were*, 'unless I were your wife'.

(iii) Accompanying a threat or an asseveration, and meaning 'if not'. Although the *Oxford English Dictionary* does not recognize this usage of *but* before 1530, there seems no doubt that it is employed at line 1243, *but I to yow be*, 'if I am not towards you', and at line 1245, *and but I be to-morn*, 'if tomorrow I am not'. The same construction appears to occur at line 1006, where it combines with a negative verb to form a double negative, thus giving emphasis to *I nam but deed*, 'if not, I shall be executed'.

NOTE ON THE TEXT

The text which follows is based upon that of F. N. Robinson (*The Complete Works of Geoffrey Chaucer*, 2nd ed., 1957). The punctuation has been revised, with special reference to the exclamation marks. Spelling has been partly rationalized, by substituting *i* for *y* wherever the change aids the modern reader and does not affect the semantic value of the word. Thus *smylyng* becomes 'smiling', and *nyghtyngale* 'nightingale', but *wyn* (wine), *lyk* (like), and *fyr* (fire) are allowed to stand.

No accentuation has been provided in this text, for two reasons. First, because it produces a page displeasing to the eye; secondly, because it no longer seems necessary or entirely reliable in the light of modern scholarship. It is not now thought that the later works of Chaucer were written in a ten-syllable line from which no variation was permissible. The correct reading of a line of Chaucer is now seen to be more closely related to the correct reading of a comparable line of prose with phrasing suited to the rhythms of speech. This allows the reader to be more flexible in interpreting the line, and makes it unreasonably pedantic to provide a rigid system of accentuation.

NOTE ON PRONUNCIATION

These equivalences are intended to offer only a rough guide.

SHORT VOWELS

$\breve{a}$ represents the sound now written *u*, as in 'cut'

$\breve{e}$ as in modern 'set'

$\breve{i}$ as in modern 'is'

$\breve{o}$ as in modern 'top'

$\breve{u}$ as in modern 'put' (not as in 'cut')

final -*e* represents the neutral vowel sound in '*a*bout' or 'atten*tio*n'. It is silent when the next word in the line begins with a vowel or an *h*.

Note on the Text

ā as in modern 'car' (not as in 'name')

ē (open—i.e. where the equivalent modern word is spelt with *ea*) as in modern 'there'

ē (close—i.e. where the equivalent modern word is spelt with *ee* or *e*) represents the sound now written *a* as in 'take'

ī as in modern 'machine' (not as in 'like')

ō (open—i.e. where the equivalent modern vowel is pronounced as in 'br*o*ther', 'm*oo*d', or 'g*oo*d') represents the sound now written *aw* as in 'fawn'

ō (close—i.e. where the equivalent modern vowel is pronounced as in 'road') as in modern 'note'

ū as in French *tu* or German *Tür*

DIPHTHONGS

ai and *ei* both roughly represent the sound now written *i* or *y* as in 'die' or 'dye'

au and *aw* both represent the sound now written *ow* or *ou* as in 'now' or 'pounce'

ou and *ow* have two pronunciations: as in *through* where the equivalent modern vowel is pronounced as in 'through' or 'mouse'; and as in *pounce* where the equivalent modern vowel is pronounced as in 'know' or 'thought'

WRITING OF VOWELS AND DIPHTHONGS

A long vowel is often indicated by doubling, as in *roote* or *eek*. The *ŭ* sound is sometimes represented by an *o* as in *yong*. The *au* sound is sometimes represented by an *a*, especially before *m* or *n*, as in *cha(u)mbre* or *cha(u)nce*.

CONSONANTS

Largely as in modern English, except that many consonants now silent were still pronounced. *Gh* was pronounced as in Scottish 'lo*ch*', and both consonants should be pronounced in such groups as the following: '*gn*acchen', '*kn*ave', '*w*ord', 'fo*lk*', '*wr*ong'.

THE PORTRAIT OF THE WIFE OF BATH

From *The General Prologue*, lines 447–78

A good WIF was ther OF biside BATHE,
But she was somdel deef, and that was scathe.
Of clooth-making she hadde swich an haunt,
She passed hem of Ypres and of Gaunt.   450
In al the parisshe wif ne was ther noon
That to the offringe bifore hire sholde goon;
And if ther dide, certeyn so wrooth was she,
That she was out of alle charitee.
Hir coverchiefs ful fine weren of ground;
I dorste swere they weyeden ten pound
That on a Sonday weren upon hir heed.
Hir hosen weren of fyn scarlet reed,
Ful streite yteyd, and shoes ful moiste and
    newe.
Boold was hir face, and fair, and reed of hewe.   460
She was a worthy womman al hir live:
Housbondes at chirche dore she hadde five,
Withouten oother compaignye in youthe,—
But therof nedeth nat to speke as nowthe.
And thries hadde she been at Jerusalem;
She hadde passed many a straunge strem;
At Rome she hadde been, and at Boloigne,
In Galice at Seint-Jame, and at Coloigne.
She koude muchel of wandringe by the weye.
Gat-tothed was she, soothly for to seye.   470
Upon an amblere esily she sat,
Ywimpled wel, and on hir heed an hat

33

As brood as is a bokeler or a targe;
A foot-mantel aboute hir hipes large,
And on hir feet a paire of spores sharpe.
In felaweshipe wel koude she laughe and carpe.
Of remedies of love she knew per chaunce,
For she koude of that art the olde daunce.

THE WIFE OF BATH'S PROLOGUE

'Experience, though noon auctoritee
Were in this world, is right ynogh for me
To speke of wo that is in mariage;
For, lordinges, sith I twelve yeer was of age,
Thonked be God that is eterne on live,
Housbondes at chirche dore I have had five—
If I so ofte mighte have ywedded bee—
And alle were worthy men in hir degree.
But me was toold, certeyn, nat longe agoon is,
That sith that Crist ne wente nevere but onis   10
To wedding, in the Cane of Galilee,
That by the same ensample taughte he me
That I ne sholde wedded be but ones.
Herkne eek, lo, which a sharp word for the nones,
Biside a welle, Jhesus, God and man,
Spak in repreeve of the Samaritan:
"Thou hast yhad five housbondes," quod he,
"And that ilke man that now hath thee
Is noght thyn housbonde," thus seyde he certeyn.
What that he mente therby, I kan nat seyn;   20
But that I axe, why that the fifthe man
Was noon housbonde to the Samaritan?
How manye mighte she have in mariage?
Yet herde I nevere tellen in myn age
Upon this nombre diffinicioun.
Men may devine and glosen, up and doun,
But wel I woot, expres, withoute lie,
God bad us for to wexe and multiplie;
That gentil text kan I wel understonde.

35

30   Eek wel I woot, he seyde myn housbonde
    Sholde lete fader and mooder, and take to me.
    But of no nombre mencion made he,
    Of bigamie, or of octogamie;
    Why sholde men thanne speke of it vileynie?
       Lo, heere, the wise king, daun Salomon;
    I trowe he hadde wives mo than oon.
    As wolde God it were leveful unto me
    To be refresshed half so ofte as he!
    Which yifte of God hadde he for alle his wives!
40   No man hath swich that in this world alive is.
    God woot, this noble king, as to my wit,
    The firste night had many a mirie fit
    With ech of hem, so wel was him on live.
    Yblessed be God that I have wedded five!
    Welcome the sixte, whan that evere he shal.
    For sothe, I wol nat kepe me chaast in al.
    Whan myn housbonde is fro the world ygon,
    Som Cristen man shal wedde me anon,
    For thanne, th'apostle seith that I am free
50   To wedde, a Goddes half, where it liketh me.
    He seith that to be wedded is no sinne;
    Bet is to be wedded than to brinne.
    What rekketh me, thogh folk seye vileynie
    Of shrewed Lameth and his bigamie?
    I woot wel Abraham was an hooly man,
    And Jacob eek, as ferforth as I kan;
    And ech of hem hadde wives mo than two,
    And many another holy man also.
    Wher can ye seye, in any manere age,
60   That hye God defended mariage
    By expres word? I pray yow, telleth me.

36

Or where comanded he virginitee?
I woot as wel as ye, it is no drede,
Th'apostel, whan he speketh of maidenhede,
He seyde that precept therof hadde he noon.
Men may conseille a womman to been oon,
But conseilling is no comandement.
He putte it in oure owene juggement;
For hadde God comanded maidenhede,
Thanne hadde he dampned wedding with the dede. 70
And certes, if ther were no seed ysowe,
Virginitee, thanne wherof sholde it growe?
Poul dorste nat comanden, atte leeste,
A thing of which his maister yaf noon heeste.
The dart is set up for virginitee:
Cacche whoso may, who renneth best lat see.
  But this word is nat taken of every wight,
But ther as God lust give it of his might.
I woot wel that th'apostel was a maide;
But nathelees, thogh that he wroot and saide   80
He wolde that every wight were swich as he,
Al nis but conseil to virginitee.
And for to been a wyf he yaf me leve
Of indulgence; so nis it no repreve
To wedde me, if that my make die,
Withouten excepcion of bigamie.
Al were it good no womman for to touche,—
He mente as in his bed or in his couche;
For peril is bothe fyr and tow t'assemble:
Ye knowe what this ensample may resemble.   90
This is al and som, he heeld virginitee
Moore parfit than wedding in freletee.
Freletee clepe I, but if that he and she

Wolde leden al hir lyf in chastitee.
  I graunte it wel, I have noon envie,
Thogh maidenhede preferre bigamie.
It liketh hem to be clene, body and goost;
Of myn estaat I nil nat make no boost.
For wel ye knowe, a lord in his houshold,
He nath nat every vessel al of gold;
Somme been of tree, and doon hir lord servise.
God clepeth folk to hym in sondry wise,
And everich hath of God a propre yifte,
Som this, som that, as him liketh shifte.
  Virginitee is greet perfeccion,
And continence eek with devocion,
But Crist, that of perfeccion is welle,
Bad nat every wight he sholde go selle
Al that he hadde, and give it to the poore
And in swich wise folwe him and his foore.
He spak to hem that wolde live parfitly;
And lordinges, by youre leve, that am nat I.
I wol bistowe the flour of al myn age
In the actes and in fruit of mariage.
  Telle me also, to what conclusion
Were membres maad of generacion,
And of so parfit wys a wight ywroght?
Trusteth right wel, they were nat maad for noght.
Glose whoso wole, and seye bothe up and doun,
That they were maked for purgacioun
Of urine, and oure bothe thinges smale
Were eek to knowe a femele from a male,
And for noon oother cause,—say ye no?
The experience woot wel it is noght so.
So that the clerkes be nat with me wrothe,

I sey this, that they maked ben for bothe,
This is to seye, for office, and for ese
Of engendrure, ther we nat God displese.
Why sholde men elles in hir bookes sette
That man shal yelde to his wyf hire dette?   130
Now wherwith sholde he make his paiement,
If he ne used his sely instrument?
Thanne were they maad upon a creature
To purge urine, and eek for engendrure.
  But I seye noght that every wight is holde,
That hath swich harneys as I to yow tolde,
To goon and usen hem in engendrure.
Thanne sholde men take of chastitee no cure.
Crist was a maide, and shapen as a man,
And many a seint, sith that the world bigan;   140
Yet lived they evere in parfit chastitee.
I nil envye no virginitee.
Lat hem be breed of pured whete-seed,
And lat us wives hoten barly-breed;
And yet with barly-breed, Mark telle kan,
Oure Lord Jhesu refresshed many a man.
In swich estaat as God hath cleped us
I wol persevere; I nam nat precius.
In wyfhod I wol use myn instrument
As frely as my Makere hath it sent.   150
If I be daungerous, God yeve me sorwe!
Myn housbonde shal it have bothe eve and morwe,
Whan that him list come forth and paye his dette.
An housbonde I wol have, I wol nat lette,
Which shal be bothe my dettour and my thral,
And have his tribulacion withal
Upon his flessh, whil that I am his wyf.

I have the power duringe al my lyf
Upon his propre body, and noght he.
160 Right thus the Apostel tolde it unto me;
And bad oure housbondes for to love us weel.
Al this sentence me liketh every deel.'

Up stirte the Pardoner, and that anon:
'Now, dame,' quod he, 'by God and by Seint John!
Ye been a noble prechour in this cas.
I was aboute to wedde a wyf; allas,
What sholde I bye it on my flessh so deere?
Yet hadde I levere wedde no wyf to-yeere!'

'Abide!' quod she, 'my tale is nat bigonne.
170 Nay, thou shalt drinken of another tonne,
Er that I go, shal savoure wors than ale.
And whan that I have toold thee forth my tale
Of tribulacion in mariage,
Of which I am expert in al myn age—
This is to seyn, myself have been the whippe—
Than maystow chese wheither thou wolt sippe
Of thilke tonne that I shal abroche.
Be war of it, er thou to ny approche;
For I shal telle ensamples mo than ten.
180 "Whoso that nil be war by othere men,
By him shul othere men corrected be."
The same wordes writeth Ptholomee;
Rede in his Almageste, and take it there.'

'Dame, I wolde praye yow, if youre wil it were,'
Seyde this Pardoner, 'as ye bigan,
Telle forth youre tale, spareth for no man,
And teche us 'yonge men of youre praktike.'

'Gladly,' quod she, 'sith it may yow like;
But that I praye to al this compaignie,

If that I speke after my fantasie,   190
As taketh not agrief of that I seye;
For myn entente is nat but for to pleye.
Now, sire, now wol I telle forth my tale.
   As evere moote I drinken wyn or ale,
I shal seye sooth, tho housbondes that I hadde,
As thre of hem were goode, and two were badde.
The thre were goode men, and riche, and olde;
Unnethe mighte they the statut holde
In which that they were bounden unto me.
Ye woot wel what I meene of this, pardee.   200
As help me God, I laughe whan I thinke
How pitously a-night I made hem swinke!
And, by my fey, I tolde of it no stoor.
They had me yeven hir lond and hir tresoor;
Me neded nat do lenger diligence
To winne hir love, or doon hem reverence.
They loved me so wel, by God above,
That I ne tolde no deyntee of hir love.
A wys womman wol bisie hire evere in oon
To gete hir love, ye, ther as she hath noon.   210
But sith I hadde hem hoolly in myn hond,
And sith they hadde me yeven al hir lond,
What sholde I taken keep hem for to plese,
But it were for my profit and myn ese?
I sette hem so a-werke, by my fey,
That many a night they songen "weilawey!"
The bacon was nat fet for hem, I trowe,
That som men han in Essex at Dunmowe.
I governed hem so wel, after my lawe,
That ech of hem ful blisful was and fawe   220
To bringe me gaye thinges fro the faire.

They were ful glad whan I spak to hem faire;
For, God it woot, I chidde hem spitously.
   Now herkneth hou I baar me proprely,
Ye wise wives, that kan understonde.
Thus shulde ye speke and bere hem wrong on honde;
For half so boldely kan ther no man
Swere and lyen, as a womman kan.
I sey nat this by wives that been wise,
230 But if it be whan they hem misavise.
A wys wyf shal, if that she kan hir good,
Bere him on honde that the cow is wood,
And take witnesse of hir owene maide
Of hir assent; but herkneth how I saide:
   "Sire olde kaynard, is this thyn array?
Why is my neighebores wyf so gay?
She is honoured over al ther she gooth;
I sitte at hoom, I have no thrifty clooth.
What dostow at my neighebores hous?
240 Is she so fair? artow so amorous?
What rowne ye with oure maide? *Benedicite!*
Sire olde lecchour, lat thy japes be.
And if I have a gossib or a freend,
Withouten gilt, thou chidest as a feend,
If that I walke or pleye unto his hous.
Thou comest hoom as dronken as a mous,
And prechest on thy bench, with ivel preef!
Thou seist to me it is a greet meschief
To wedde a povre womman, for costage;
250 And if that she be riche, of heigh parage,
Thanne seistow that it is a tormentrie
To soffre hire pride and hire malencolie.
And if that she be fair, thou verray knave,

Thou seist that every holour wol hire have;
She may no while in chastitee abide,
That is assailled upon ech a side.

Thou seist som folk desiren us for richesse,
Somme for oure shap, and somme for oure fairnesse,
And som for she kan outher singe or daunce,
And som for gentillesse and daliaunce;   260
Som for hir handes and hir armes smale:
Thus goth al to the devel, by thy tale.
Thou seist men may nat kepe a castel wal,
It may so longe assailled been overal.

And if that she be foul, thou seist that she
Coveiteth every man that she may se,
For as a spaynel she wol on him lepe,
Til that she finde som man hire to chepe.
Ne noon so grey goos gooth ther in the lake
As, sëistow, wol been withoute make.   270
And seist it is an hard thing for to welde
A thing that no man wole, his thankes, helde.
Thus seistow, lorel, whan thow goost to bedde;
And that no wys man nedeth for to wedde,
Ne no man that entendeth unto hevene.
With wilde thonder-dint and firy levene
Moote thy welked nekke be tobroke!

Thow seist that dropping houses, and eek smoke,
And chiding wives maken men to flee
Out of hir owene hous; a, *benedicitee!*   280
What eyleth swich an old man for to chide?

Thow seist we wives wol oure vices hide
Til we be fast, and thanne we wol hem shewe—
Wel may that be a proverbe of a shrewe!

Thou seist that oxen, asses, hors, and houndes,

They been assayed at diverse stoundes;
Bacins, lavours, er that men hem bye,
Spoones and stooles, and al swich housbondrie,
And so been pottes, clothes, and array;
290 But folk of wives maken noon assay,
Til they be wedded; olde dotard shrewe!
And thanne, seistow, we wol oure vices shewe.

Thou seist also that it displeseth me
But if that thou wolt preyse my beautee,
And but thou poure alwey upon my face,
And clepe me 'faire dame' in every place.
And but thou make a feeste on thilke day
That I was born, and make me fressh and gay;
And but thou do to my norice honour,
300 And to my chamberere withinne my bour,
And to my fadres folk and his allies—
Thus seistow, olde barel-ful of lies!

And yet of oure apprentice Janekin,
For his crispe heer, shininge as gold so fyn,
And for he squiereth me bothe up and doun,
Yet hastow caught a fals suspecioun.
I wol him noght, thogh thou were deed tomorwe!

But tel me this: why hidestow, with sorwe,
The keyes of thy cheste awey fro me?
310 It is my good as wel as thyn, pardee!
What, wenestow make an idiot of oure dame?
Now by that lord that called is Seint Jame,
Thou shalt nat bothe, thogh that thou were wood,
Be maister of my body and of my good;
That oon thou shalt forgo, maugree thine yen.
What helpith it of me to enquere or spyen?
I trowe thou woldest loke me in thy chiste!

44

Thou sholdest seye, 'Wyf, go wher thee liste;
Taak youre disport, I wol nat leve no talis.
I knowe yow for a trewe wyf, dame Alis.'   320
We love no man that taketh kep or charge
Wher that we goon; we wol ben at oure large.

    Of alle men yblessed moot he be,
The wise astrologien, Daun Ptholome,
That seith this proverbe in his Almageste:
'Of alle men his wisdom is the hyeste
That rekketh nevere who hath the world in honde.'
By this proverbe thou shalt understonde,
Have thou ynogh, what thar thee recche or care
How mirily that othere folkes fare?   330
For, certeyn, olde dotard, by youre leve,
Ye shul have queynte right ynogh at eve.
He is to greet a nigard that wolde werne
A man to lighte a candle at his lanterne;
He shal have never the lasse light, pardee.
Have thou ynogh, thee thar nat pleyne thee.

    Thou seist also, that if we make us gay
With clothing, and with precious array,
That it is peril of oure chastitee;
And yet, with sorwe! thou most enforce thee,   340
And seye thise wordes in the Apostles name:
'In habit maad with chastitee and shame
Ye wommen shul apparaille yow,' quod he,
'And noght in tressed heer and gay perree,
As perles, ne with gold, ne clothes riche.'
After thy text, ne after thy rubriche,
I wol nat wirche as muchel as a gnat.

    Thou seydest this, that I was lyk a cat;
For whoso wolde senge a cattes skin,

350 Thanne wolde the cat wel dwellen in his in;
And if the cattes skin be slik and gay,
She wol nat dwelle in house half a day,
But forth she wole, er any day be dawed,
To shewe hir skin, and goon a-caterwawed.
This is to seye, if I be gay, sire shrewe,
I wol renne out, my borel for to shewe.

Sire olde fool, what helpeth thee to spyen?
Thogh thou preye Argus with his hundred yen
To be my warde-cors, as he kan best,
360 In feith, he shal nat kepe me but me lest;
Yet koude I make his berd, so moot I thee!

Thou seydest eek that ther been thinges thre,
The whiche thinges troublen al this erthe,
And that no wight may endure the ferthe.
O leeve sire shrewe, Jhesu shorte thy lyf!
Yet prechestow and seist an hateful wyf
Yrekened is for oon of thise meschances.
Been ther none othere maner resemblances
That ye may likne youre parables to,
370 But if a sely wyf be oon of tho?

Thou liknest eek wommenes love to helle,
To bareyne lond, ther water may nat dwelle.
Thou liknest it also to wilde fyr;
The moore it brenneth, the moore it hath desir
To consume every thing that brent wole be.
Thou seyest, right as wormes shende a tree,
Right so a wyf destroyeth hire housbonde;
This knowe they that been to wives bonde."

Lordinges, right thus, as ye have understonde,
380 Baar I stifly mine olde housbondes on honde
That thus they seyden in hir dronkenesse;

46

And al was fals, but that I took witnesse
On Janekin, and on my nece also.
O Lord! the peyne I dide hem and the wo,
Ful giltelees, by Goddes sweete pine!
For as an hors I koude bite and whine.
I koude pleyne, and yit was in the gilt,
Or elles often time hadde I been spilt.
Whoso that first to mille comth, first grint;
I pleyned first, so was oure werre ystint. 390
They were ful glade to excuse hem blive
Of thing of which they nevere agilte hir live.
Of wenches wolde I beren hem on honde,
Whan that for sik unnethes mighte they stonde.
   Yet tikled I his herte, for that he
Wende that I hadde of him so greet chiertee.
I swoor that al my walkinge out by nighte
Was for t'espie wenches that he dighte;
Under that colour hadde I many a mirthe.
For al swich wit is yeven us in oure birthe; 400
Deceite, weping, spinning God hath yive
To wommen kindely, whil that they may live.
And thus of o thing I avaunte me,
Atte ende I hadde the bettre in ech degree,
By sleighte, or force, or by som maner thing,
As by continueel murmur or grucching.
Namely abedde hadden they meschaunce:
Ther wolde I chide, and do hem no plesaunce;
I wolde no lenger in the bed abide,
If that I felte his arm over my side, 410
Til he had maad his raunson unto me;
Thanne wolde I suffre him do his nicetee.
And therfore every man this tale I telle,

Winne whoso may, for al is for to selle;
With empty hand men may none haukes lure.
For winning wolde I al his lust endure,
And make me a feyned appetit;
And yet in bacon hadde I nevere delit;
That made me that evere I wolde hem chide.
420 For thogh the pope hadde seten hem biside,
I wolde nat spare hem at hir owene bord;
For, by my trouthe, I quitte hem word for word.
As helpe me verray God omnipotent,
Though I right now sholde make my testament,
I ne owe hem nat a word that it nis quit.
I broghte it so aboute by my wit
That they moste yeve it up, as for the beste,
Or elles hadde we nevere been in reste.
For thogh he looked as a wood leon,
430 Yet sholde he faille of his conclusion.
    Thanne wolde I seye, "Goode lief, taak keep
How mekely looketh Wilkin, oure sheep!
Com neer, my spouse, lat me ba thy cheke!
Ye sholde been al pacient and meke,
And han a sweete spiced conscience,
Sith ye so preche of Jobes pacience.
Suffreth alwey, sin ye so wel kan preche;
And but ye do, certein we shal yow teche
That it is fair to have a wyf in pees.
440 Oon of us two moste bowen, doutelees;
And sith a man is moore resonable
Than womman is, ye moste been suffrable.
What eyleth yow to grucche thus and grone?
Is it for ye wolde have my queynte allone?
Wy, taak it al! lo, have it every deel!

48

Peter! I shrewe yow, but ye love it weel;
For if I wolde selle my *bele chose*,
I koude walke as fressh as is a rose;
But I wol kepe it for youre owene tooth.
Ye be to blame, by God! I sey yow sooth." 450
    Swiche manere wordes hadde we on honde.
Now wol I speken of my fourthe housbonde.

    My fourthe housbonde was a revelour;
This is to seyn, he hadde a paramour;
And I was yong and ful of ragerie,
Stibourn and strong, and joly as a pie.
How koude I daunce to an harpe smale,
And singe, ywis, as any nightingale,
Whan I had dronke a draughte of sweete wyn!
Metellius, the foule cherl, the swyn, 460
That with a staf birafte his wyf hir lyf,
For she drank wyn, thogh I hadde been his wyf,
He sholde nat han daunted me fro drinke!
And after wyn on Venus moste I thinke,
For al so siker as cold engendreth hail,
A likerous mouth moste han a likerous tail.
In wommen vinolent is no defence,—
This knowen lecchours by experience.

    But, Lord Crist! whan that it remembreth me
Upon my yowthe, and on my jolitee, 470
It tikleth me aboute myn herte roote.
Unto this day it dooth myn herte boote
That I have had my world as in my time.
But age, allas, that al wole envenime,
Hath me biraft my beautee and my pith.
Lat go, farewel; the devel go therwith!
The flour is goon, ther is namoore to telle;

The bren, as I best kan, now moste I selle;
But yet to be right mirie wol I fonde.

480   Now wol I tellen of my fourthe housbonde.
    I seye, I hadde in herte greet despit
That he of any oother had delit.
But he was quit, by God and by Seint Joce!
I made him of the same wode a croce;
Nat of my body, in no foul manere,
But certeinly, I made folk swich cheere
That in his owene grece I made him frie
For angre, and for verray jalousie.
By God! in erthe I was his purgatorie,

490   For which I hope his soule be in glorie.
For, God it woot, he sat ful ofte and song,
Whan that his shoo ful bitterly him wrong.
Ther was no wight, save God and he, that wiste,
In many wise, how soore I him twiste.
He deyde whan I cam fro Jerusalem,
And lith ygrave under the roode beem,
Al is his tombe noght so curius
As was the sepulcre of him Darius,
Which that Appelles wroghte subtilly;

500   It nis but wast to burye him preciously.
Lat him fare wel, God yeve his soul reste!
He is now in his grave and in his cheste.
    Now of my fifthe housbonde wol I telle.
God lete his soule nevere come in helle!
And yet was he to me the mooste shrewe;
That feele I on my ribbes al by rewe,
And evere shal unto myn ending day.
But in oure bed he was so fressh and gay,
And therwithal so wel koude he me glose,

Whan that he wolde han my *bele chose*,   510
That thogh he hadde me bete on every bon,
He koude winne again my love anon.
I trowe I loved him best, for that he
Was of his love daungerous to me.
We wommen han, if that I shal nat lie,
In this matere a queynte fantasie;
Waite what thing we may nat lightly have,
Therafter wol we crie al day and crave.
Forbede us thing, and that desiren we;
Preesse on us faste, and thanne wol we fle.   520
With daunger oute we al oure chaffare;
Greet prees at market maketh deere ware,
And to greet cheep is holde at litel prys:
This knoweth every womman that is wys.

   My fifthe housbonde, God his soule blesse!
Which that I took for love, and no richesse,
He som time was a clerk of Oxenford,
And hadde left scole, and wente at hom to bord
With my gossib, dwellinge in oure toun;
God have hir soule! hir name was Alisoun.   530
She knew myn herte, and eek my privetee,
Bet than oure parisshe preest, so moot I thee!
To hire biwreyed I my conseil al.
For hadde myn housbonde pissed on a wal,
Or doon a thyng that sholde han cost his lyf,
To hire, and to another worthy wyf,
And to my nece, which that I loved weel,
I wolde han toold his conseil every deel.
And so I dide ful often, God it woot,
That made his face often reed and hoot   540
For verray shame, and blamed himself for he

Had toold to me so greet a privetee.
  And so bifel that ones in a Lente—
So often times I to my gossib wente,
For evere yet I loved to be gay,
And for to walke in March, Averill, and May,
Fro hous to hous, to heere sondry talis—
That Jankin clerk, and my gossib dame Alis,
And I myself, into the feeldes wente.
550 Myn housbonde was at Londoun al that Lente;
I hadde the bettre leyser for to pleye,
And for to se, and eek for to be seye
Of lusty folk. What wiste I wher my grace
Was shapen for to be, or in what place?
Therfore I made my visitaciouns
To vigilies and to processiouns,
To preching eek, and to thise pilgrimages,
To pleyes of miracles, and to mariages,
And wered upon my gaye scarlet gites.
560 Thise wormes, ne thise motthes, ne thise mites,
Upon my peril, frete hem never a deel;
And wostow why? for they were used weel.
  Now wol I tellen forth what happed me.
I seye that in the feeldes walked we,
Til trewely we hadde swich daliance,
This clerk and I, that of my purveiance
I spak to him and seyde him how that he,
If I were widwe, sholde wedde me.
For certeinly, I sey for no bobance,
570 Yet was I nevere withouten purveiance
Of mariage, n'of othere thinges eek.
I holde a mouses herte nat worth a leek
That hath but oon hole for to sterte to,

And if that faille, thanne is al ydo.

    I bar hym on honde he hadde enchanted me,—
My dame taughte me that soutiltee.
And eek I seyde I mette of him al night,
He wolde han slain me as I lay upright,
And al my bed was ful of verray blood;
But yet I hope that he shal do me good,   580
For blood bitokeneth gold, as me was taught.
And al was fals; I dremed of it right naught,
But as I folwed ay my dames loore,
As wel of this as of othere thinges moore.

    But now, sire, lat me se, what I shal seyn?
A ha! by God, I have my tale ageyn.

    Whan that my fourthe housbonde was on beere,
I weep algate, and made sory cheere,
As wives mooten, for it is usage,
And with my coverchief covered my visage,   590
But for that I was purveyed of a make,
I wepte but smal, and that I undertakè.

    To chirche was myn housbonde born a-morwe
With neighebores, that for him maden sorwe;
And Jankin, oure clerk, was oon of tho.
As help me God! whan that I saugh him go
After the beere, me thoughte he hadde a paire
Of legges and of feet so clene and faire
That al myn herte I yaf unto his hoold.
He was, I trowe, a twenty winter oold,   600
And I was fourty, if I shal seye sooth;
But yet I hadde alwey a coltes tooth.
Gat-tothed I was, and that bicam me weel;
I hadde the prente of seinte Venus seel.
As help me God! I was a lusty oon,

And faire, and riche, and yong, and wel bigon;
And trewely, as mine housbondes tolde me,
I hadde the beste *quoniam* mighte be.
For certes, I am al Venerien
610   In feelinge, and myn herte is Marcien.
Venus me yaf my lust, my likerousnesse,
And Mars yaf me my sturdy hardinesse;
Myn ascendent was Taur, and Mars therinne.
Allas, allas, that evere love was sinne!
I folwed ay myn inclinacioun
By vertu of my constellacioun;
That made me I koude noght withdrawe
My chambre of Venus from a good felawe.
Yet have I Martes mark upon my face,
620   And also in another privee place.
For God so wys be my savacioun,
I ne loved nevere by no discrecioun,
But evere folwede myn appetit,
Al were he short, or long, or blak, or whit;
I took no kep, so that he liked me,
How poore he was, ne eek of what degree.
    What sholde I seye? but, at the monthes ende,
This joly clerk, Jankin, that was so hende,
Hath wedded me with greet solempnitee;
630   And to him yaf I al the lond and fee
That evere was me yeven therbifoore.
But afterward repented me ful soore;
He nolde suffre nothing of my list.
By God! he smoot me ones on the list,
For that I rente out of his book a leef,
That of the strook myn ere wax al deef.
Stibourn I was as is a leonesse,

And of my tonge a verray jangleresse,
And walke I wolde, as I had doon biforn,
From hous to hous, although he had it sworn;   640
For which he often times wolde preche,
And me of olde Romain geestes teche;
How he Simplicius Gallus lefte his wyf,
And hire forsook for terme of al his lyf,
Noght but for open-heveded he hir say
Lookinge out at his dore upon a day.

   Another Romain tolde he me by name,
That, for his wyf was at a someres game
Withouten his witing, he forsook hire eke.
And thanne wolde he upon his Bible seke   650
That ilke proverbe of Ecclesiaste
Where he comandeth, and forbedeth faste,
Man shal nat suffre his wyf go roule aboute.
Thanne wolde he seye right thus, withouten doute:
   "Whoso that buildeth his hous al of salwes,
And priketh his blinde hors over the falwes,
And suffreth his wyf to go seken halwes,
Is worthy to been hanged on the galwes!"
But al for noght, I sette noght an hawe
Of his proverbes n'of his olde sawe,   660
Ne I wolde nat of him corrected be.
I hate him that my vices telleth me,
And so doo mo, God woot, of us than I.
This made him with me wood al outrely;
I nolde noght forbere him in no cas.

   Now wol I sey yow sooth, by Seint Thomas,
Why that I rente out of his book a leef,
For which he smoot me so that I was deef.
   He hadde a book that gladly, night and day,

670   For his desport he wolde rede alway;
He cleped it Valerie and Theofraste,
At which book he lough alwey ful faste.
And eek ther was somtime a clerk at Rome,
A cardinal, that highte Seint Jerome,
That made a book again Jovinian;
In which book eek ther was Tertulan,
Crisippus, Trotula, and Helowis,
That was abbesse nat fer fro Paris;
And eek the Parables of Salomon,
680   Ovides Art, and bookes many on,
And alle thise were bounden in o volume.
And every night and day was his custume,
Whan he hadde leyser and vacacioun
From oother worldly occupacioun,
To reden on this book of wikked wives.
He knew of hem mo legendes and lives
Than been of goode wives in the Bible.
For trusteth wel, it is an impossible
That any clerk wol speke good of wives,
690   But if it be of hooly seintes lives,
Ne of noon oother womman never the mo.
Who peyntede the leon, tel me who?
By God! if wommen hadde writen stories,
As clerkes han withinne hire oratories,
They wolde han writen of men moore wikkednesse
Than al the mark of Adam may redresse.
The children of Mercurie and of Venus
Been in hir wirking ful contrarius;
Mercurie loveth wisdam and science,
700   And Venus loveth riot and dispence.
And, for hire diverse disposicioun,

56

Ech falleth in otheres exaltacioun.
And thus, God woot, Mercurie is desolat
In Pisces, wher Venus is exaltat;
And Venus falleth ther Mercurie is reysed.
Therfore no womman of no clerk is preysed.
The clerk, whan he is oold, and may noght do
Of Venus werkes worth his olde sho,
Thanne sit he doun, and writ in his dotage
That wommen kan nat kepe hir mariage.　　　　710

　　But now to purpos, why I tolde thee
That I was beten for a book, pardee!
Upon a night Jankin, that was oure sire,
Redde on his book, as he sat by the fire,
Of Eva first, that for hir wikkednesse
Was al mankinde broght to wrecchednesse,
For which that Jhesu Crist himself was slain,
That boghte us with his herte blood again.
Lo, heere expres of womman may ye finde,
That womman was the los of al mankinde.　　　　720

　　Tho redde he me how Sampson loste his heres:
Slepinge, his lemman kitte it with hir sheres;
Thurgh which treson loste he bothe his yen.

　　Tho redde he me, if that I shal nat lyen,
Of Hercules and of his Dianire,
That caused hym to sette hymself afire.

　　No thing forgat he the care and the wo
That Socrates hadde with his wives two;
How Xantippa caste pisse upon his heed.
This sely man sat stille as he were deed;　　　　730
He wiped his heed, namoore dorste he seyn,
But "Er that thonder stinte, comth a reyn!"

　　Of Phasipha, that was the queene of Crete,

For shrewednesse, him thoughte the tale swete;
Fy! spek namoore—it is a grisly thyng—
Of hire horrible lust and hir liking.
      Of Clitermystra, for hire lecherie,
That falsly made hire housbonde for to die,
He redde it with ful good devocioun.
      He tolde me eek for what occasioun
Amphiorax at Thebes loste his lyf.
Myn housbonde hadde a legende of his wyf,
Eriphilem, that for an ouche of gold
Hath prively unto the Grekes told
Wher that hir housbonde hidde him in a place,
For which he hadde at Thebes sory grace.
      Of Livia tolde he me, and of Lucie:
They bothe made hir housbondes for to die;
That oon for love, that oother was for hate.
      Livia hir housbonde, on an even late,
Empoisoned hath, for that she was his fo;
Lucia, likerous, loved hire housbonde so
That, for he sholde alwey upon hire thinke,
She yaf him swich a manere love-drinke
That he was deed er it were by the morwe;
And thus algates housbondes han sorwe.
      Thanne tolde he me how oon Latumius
Compleyned unto his felawe Arrius
That in his gardin growed swich a tree
On which he seyde how that his wives thre
Hanged hemself for herte despitus.
"O leeve brother," quod this Arrius,
"Yif me a plante of thilke blissed tree,
And in my gardin planted shal it bee."
      Of latter date, of wives hath he red

740

750

760

That somme han slain hir housbondes in hir bed,
And lete hir lecchour dighte hire al the night,
Whan that the corps lay in the floor upright.
And somme han drive nailes in hir brain,
Whil that they slepte, and thus they had hem slain. 770
Somme han hem yeve poisoun in hire drinke.
He spak moore harm than herte may bithinke;
And therwithal he knew of mo proverbes
Than in this world ther growen gras or herbes.
"Bet is," quod he, "thyn habitacioun
Be with a leon or a foul dragoun,
Than with a womman usinge for to chide."
"Bet is," quod he, "hye in the roof abide,
Than with an angry wyf doun in the hous;
They been so wikked and contrarious,   780
They haten that hir housbondes loven ay."
He seyde, "a womman cast hir shame away,
Whan she cast of hir smok"; and forthermo,
"A fair womman, but she be chaast also,
Is lyk a gold ring in a sowes nose."
Who wolde wene, or who wolde suppose,
The wo that in myn herte was, and pine?
    And whan I saugh he wolde nevere fine
To reden on this cursed book al night,
Al sodeynly thre leves have I plight   790
Out of his book, right as he radde, and eke
I with my fest so took him on the cheke
That in oure fyr he fil bakward adoun.
And he up stirte as dooth a wood leoun,
And with his fest he smoot me on the heed,
That in the floor I lay as I were deed.
And whan he saugh how stille that I lay,

He was agast, and wolde han fled his way,
Til atte laste out of my swogh I breyde.
800 "O, hastow slain me, false theef?" I seyde,
"And for my land thus hastow mordred me?
Er I be deed, yet wol I kisse thee."

    And neer he cam, and kneled faire adoun,
And seyde, "Deere suster Alisoun,
As help me God! I shal thee nevere smite.
That I have doon, it is thyself to wite.
Foryeve it me, and that I thee biseke!"
And yet eftsoones I hitte him on the cheke,
And seyde, "Theef, thus muchel am I wreke;
810 Now wol I die, I may no lenger speke."
But atte laste, with muchel care and wo,
We fille acorded by us selven two.
He yaf me al the bridel in myn hond,
To han the governance of hous and lond,
And of his tonge, and of his hond also;
And made him brenne his book anon right tho.
And whan that I hadde geten unto me,
By maistrie, al the soverainetee,
And that he seyde, "Myn owene trewe wyf,
820 Do as thee lust the terme of al thy lyf;
Keep thyn honour, and keep eek myn estaat"—
After that day we hadden never debaat.
God helpe me so, I was to him as kinde
As any wyf from Denmark unto Inde,
And also trewe, and so was he to me.
I prey to God, that sit in magestee,
So blesse his soule for his mercy deere.
Now wol I seye my tale, if ye wol heere.'

    The Frere lough, whan he hadde herd al this;

'Now dame,' quod he, 'so have I joye or blis, 830
This is a long preamble of a tale!'
And whan the Somonour herde the Frere gale,
'Lo,' quod the Somonour, 'Goddes armes two!
A frere wol entremette him everemo.
Lo, goode men, a flie and eek a frere
Wol falle in every dissh and eek mateere.
What spekestow of preambulacioun?
What! amble, or trotte, or pees, or go sit doun!
Thou lettest oure disport in this manere.'
    'Ye, woltow so, sire Somonour?' quod the Frere; 840
'Now, by my feith, I shal, er that I go,
Telle of a somonour swich a tale or two,
That alle the folk shal laughen in this place.'
    'Now elles, Frere, I bishrewe thy face,'
Quod this Somonour, 'and I bishrewe me,
But if I telle tales two or thre
Of freres, er I come to Sidingborne,
That I shal make thyn herte for to morne,
For wel I woot thy pacience is gon.'
    Oure Hooste cride 'Pees! and that anon!' 850
And seyde, 'Lat the womman telle hire tale.
Ye fare as folk that dronken ben of ale.
Do, dame, telle forth youre tale, and that is best.'
    'Al redy, sire,' quod she, 'right as yow lest,
If I have licence of this worthy Frere.'
    'Yis, dame,' quod he, 'tel forth, and I wol heere.'

THE WIFE OF BATH'S TALE

In th'olde dayes of the King Arthour,
Of which that Britons speken greet honour,
Al was this land fulfild of faierie.
The elf-queene, with hir joly compaignie,   860
Daunced ful ofte in many a grene mede.
This was the olde opinion, as I rede;
I speke of manie hundred yeres ago.
But now kan no man se none elves mo,
For now the grete charitee and prayeres
Of limitours and othere hooly freres,
That serchen every lond and every streem,
As thikke as motes in the sonne-beem,
Blessinge halles, chambres, kichenes, boures,
Citees, burghes, castels, hye toures,   870
Thropes, bernes, shipnes, daieries—
This maketh that ther ben no faieries.
For ther as wont to walken was an elf,
Ther walketh now the limitour himself,
In undermeles and in morweninges,
And seyth his matins and his hooly thinges
As he gooth in his limitacioun.
Wommen may go now saufly up and doun.
In every bussh or under every tree
Ther is noon oother incubus but he,   880
And he ne wol doon hem but dishonour.
    And so bifel it that this king Arthour
Hadde in his hous a lusty bacheler,
That on a day cam ridinge fro river;
And happed that, allone as he was born,

He saugh a maide walkinge him biforn,
Of which maide anon, maugree hir heed,
By verray force, he rafte hire maidenhed;
For which oppressioun was swich clamour
890   And swich pursute unto the king Arthour,
That dampned was this knight for to be deed,
By cours of lawe, and sholde han lost his heed—
Paraventure swich was the statut tho—
But that the queene and othere ladies mo
So longe preyeden the king of grace,
Til he his lyf him graunted in the place,
And yaf him to the queene, al at hir wille,
To chese wheither she wolde him save or spille.

The queene thanketh the king with al hir might,
900   And after this thus spak she to the knight,
Whan that she saugh hir time, upon a day:
'Thou standest yet,' quod she, 'in swich array
That of thy lyf yet hastow no suretee.
I grante thee lyf, if thou kanst tellen me
What thing is it that wommen moost desiren.
Be war, and keep thy nekke-boon from iren!
And if thou kanst nat tellen it anon,
Yet wol I yeve thee leve for to gon
A twelf-month and a day, to seche and leere
910   An answere suffisant in this mateere;
And suretee wol I han, er that thou pace,
Thy body for to yelden in this place.'

Wo was this knight, and sorwefully he siketh;
But what, he may nat do al as him liketh.
And at the laste he chees him for to wende,
And come again, right at the yeres ende,
With swich answere as God wolde him purveye;

64

And taketh his leve, and wendeth forth his weye.
  He seketh every hous and every place
Where as he hopeth for to finde grace,   920
To lerne what thing wommen loven moost;
But he ne koude arriven in no coost
Wher as he mighte finde in this mateere
Two creatures accordinge in-feere.
Somme seyde wommen loven best richesse,
Somme seyde honour, somme seyde jolinesse,
Somme riche array, somme seyden lust abedde,
And oftetime to be widwe and wedde.
Somme seyde that oure hertes been moost esed
Whan that we been yflatered and yplesed.   930
He gooth ful ny the sothe, I wol nat lie.
A man shal winne us best with flaterie;
And with attendance, and with bisinesse,
Been we ylimed, bothe moore and lesse.
  And somme seyen that we loven best
For to be free, and do right as us lest,
And that no man repreve us of oure vice,
But seye that we be wise, and no thing nice.
For trewely ther is noon of us alle,
If any wight wol clawe us on the galle,   940
That we nel kike, for he seith us sooth.
Assay, and he shal finde it that so dooth;
For, be we never so vicious withinne,
We wol been holden wise and clene of sinne.
  And somme seyn that greet delit han we
For to been holden stable, and eek secree,
And in o purpos stedefastly to dwelle,
And nat biwreye thing that men us telle.
But that tale is nat worth a rake-stele.

950 Pardee, we wommen konne no thing hele;
Witnesse on Mida,—wol ye heere the tale?

Ovide, amonges othere thinges smale,
Seyde Mida hadde, under his longe heres,
Growinge upon his heed two asses eres,
The whiche vice he hidde, as he best mighte,
Ful subtilly from every mannes sighte,
That, save his wyf, ther wiste of it namo.
He loved hire moost, and trusted hire also;
He preyede hire that to no creature
960 She sholde tellen of his disfigure.

She swoor him nay, for al this world to winne,
She nolde do that vileynie or sinne,
To make hir housbonde han so foul a name.
She nolde nat telle it for hir owene shame.
But nathelees, hir thoughte that she dide,
That she so longe sholde a conseil hide;
Hir thoughte it swal so soore aboute hir herte
That nedely som word hire moste asterte;
And sith she dorste telle it to no man,
970 Doun to a mareys faste by she ran—
Til she cam there, hir herte was a-fire—
And as a bitore bombleth in the mire,
She leyde hir mouth unto the water doun:
'Biwreye me nat, thou water, with thy soun,'
Quod she; 'to thee I telle it and namo;
Myn housbonde hath longe asses eris two!
Now is myn herte al hool, now is it oute.
I myghte no lenger kepe it, out of doute.'
Heere may ye se, thogh we a time abide,
980 Yet out it moot; we kan no conseil hide.
The remenant of the tale if ye wol heere,

66

Redeth Ovide, and ther ye may it leere.
  This knight, of which my tale is specially,
Whan that he saugh he mighte nat come therby—
This is to seye, what wommen love moost—
Withinne his brest ful sorweful was the goost.
But hoom he gooth, he mighte nat sojourne;
The day was come that homward moste he tourne.
And in his wey it happed him to ride,
In al this care, under a forest side,   990
Wher as he saugh upon a daunce go
Of ladies foure and twenty, and yet mo;
Toward the whiche daunce he drow ful yerne,
In hope that som wisdom sholde he lerne.
But certeinly, er he cam fully there,
Vanisshed was this daunce, he niste where.
No creature saugh he that bar lyf,
Save on the grene he saugh sittinge a wyf;
A fouler wight ther may no man devise.
Again the knight this olde wyf gan rise,   1000
And seyde, 'Sire knight, heer forth ne lith no wey.
Tel me what that ye seken, by youre fey!
Paraventure it may the bettre be;
Thise olde folk kan muchel thing,' quod she.
  'My leeve mooder,' quod this knight, 'certeyn
I nam but deed, but if that I kan seyn
What thing it is that wommen moost desire.
Koude ye me wisse, I wolde wel quite youre hire.'
  'Plight me thy trouthe heere in myn hand,' quod she,
'The nexte thing that I requere thee,   1010
Thou shalt it do, if it lie in thy might,
And I wol telle it yow er it be night.'
  'Have heer my trouthe,' quod the knight, 'I grante.'

67

'Thanne,' quod she, 'I dar me wel avante
Thy lyf is sauf; for I wol stonde therby,
Upon my lyf, the queene wol seye as I.
Lat se which is the proudeste of hem alle,
That wereth on a coverchief or a calle,
That dar seye nay of that I shal thee teche.
1020 Lat us go forth, withouten lenger speche.'
Tho rowned she a pistel in his ere,
And bad him to be glad, and have no fere.

Whan they be comen to the court, this knight
Seyde he had holde his day, as he hadde hight,
And redy was his answere, as he sayde.
Ful many a noble wyf, and many a maide,
And many a widwe, for that they been wise,
The queene hirself sittinge as a justise,
Assembled been, his answere for to heere;
1030 And afterward this knight was bode appeere.

To every wight comanded was silence,
And that the knight sholde telle in audience
What thing that worldly wommen loven best.
This knight ne stood nat stille as doth a best,
But to his questioun anon answerde
With manly vois, that al the court it herde:
'My lige lady, generally,' quod he,
'Wommen desiren to have sovereinetee
As wel over hir housbond as hir love,
1040 And for to been in maistrie him above.
This is youre mooste desir, thogh ye me kille.
Dooth as yow list; I am heer at youre wille.'
In al the court ne was ther wyf, ne maide,
Ne widwe, that contraried that he saide,
But seyden he was worthy han his lyf.

And with that word up stirte the olde wyf,
Which that the knight saugh sittinge on the grene:
'Mercy,' quod she, 'my soverein lady queene!
Er that youre court departe, do me right.
I taughte this answere unto the knight;   1050
For which he plighte me his trouthe there,
The firste thing that I wolde him requere,
He wolde it do, if it lay in his might.
Bifore the court thanne preye I thee, sir knight,'
Quod she, 'that thou me take unto thy wyf;
For wel thou woost that I have kept thy lyf.
If I seye fals, sey nay, upon thy fey!'

   This knight answerde, 'Allas, and weilawey!
I woot right wel that swich was my biheste.
For Goddes love, as chees a newe requeste;   1060
Taak al my good, and lat my body go.'

   'Nay, thanne,' quod she, 'I shrewe us bothe two!
For thogh that I be foul, and oold, and poore,
I nolde for al the metal, ne for oore,
That under erthe is grave, or lith above,
But if thy wyf I were, and eek thy love.'

   'My love?' quod he, 'nay, my dampnacioun!
Allas, that any of my nacioun
Sholde evêre so foule disparaged be!'
But al for noght; the ende is this, that he   1070
Constreined was, he nedes moste hire wedde;
And taketh his olde wyf, and gooth to bedde.

   Now wolden som men seye, paraventure,
That for my necligence I do no cure
To tellen yow the joye and al th'array
That at the feeste was that ilke day.
To which thing shortly answeren I shal:

I seye ther nas no joye ne feeste at al;
Ther nas but hevinesse and muche sorwe.
1080 For prively he wedded hire on the morwe,
And al day after hidde him as an owle,
So wo was him, his wyf looked so foule.

Greet was the wo the knight hadde in his thoght,
Whan he was with his wyf abedde ybroght;
He walweth and he turneth to and fro.
His olde wyf lay smilinge everemo,
And seyde, 'O deere housbonde, *benedicitee!*
Fareth every knight thus with his wyf as ye?
Is this the lawe of King Arthures hous?
1090 Is every knight of his so dangerous?
I am youre owene love and eek youre wyf;
I am she which that saved hath youre lyf,
And, certes, yet ne dide I yow nevere unright;
Why fare ye thus with me this firste night?
Ye faren lyk a man had lost his wit.
What is my gilt? For Goddes love, tel me it,
And it shal been amended, if I may.'

'Amended?' quod this knight, 'allas, nay, nay!
It wol nat been amended nevere mo.
1100 Thou art so loothly, and so oold also,
And therto comen of so lough a kinde,
That litel wonder is thogh I walwe and winde.
So wolde God myn herte wolde breste!'
'Is this,' quod she, 'the cause of youre unreste?'
'Ye, certeinly,' quod he, 'no wonder is.'
'Now, sire,' quod she, 'I koude amende al this,
If that me liste, er it were dayes thre,
So wel ye mighte bere yow unto me.
But, for ye speken of swich gentillesse

As is descended out of old richesse,   1110
That therfore sholden ye be gentil men,
Swich arrogance is nat worth an hen.
Looke who that is moost vertuous alway,
Privee and apert, and moost entendeth ay
To do the gentil dedes that he kan;
Taak him for the grettest gentil man.
Crist wole we claime of him oure gentillesse,
Nat of oure eldres for hire old richesse.
For thogh they yeve us al hir heritage,
For which we claime to been of heigh parage,   1120
Yet may they nat biquethe, for no thing,
To noon of us hir vertuous living,
That made hem gentil men ycalled be,
And bad us folwen hem in swich degree.

   Wel kan the wise poete of Florence,
That highte Dant, speken in this sentence.
Lo, in swich maner rym is Dantes tale:
"Ful selde up riseth by his branches smale
Prowesse of man, for God, of his goodnesse,
Wole that of him we claime oure gentillesse";   1130
For of oure eldres may we no thing claime
But temporel thing, that man may hurte and maime.

   Eek every wight woot this as wel as I,
If gentillesse were planted natureelly
Unto a certeyn linage doun the line,
Privee and apert, thanne wolde they nevere fine
To doon of gentillesse the faire office;
They mighte do no vileynie or vice.

   Taak fyr, and ber it in the derkeste hous
Bitwix this and the mount of Kaukasous,   1140
And lat men shette the dores and go thenne;

71

Yet wole the fyr as faire lie and brenne
As twenty thousand men mighte it biholde;
His office natureel ay wol it holde,
Up peril of my lyf, til that it die.
　Heere may ye se wel how that genterie
Is nat annexed to possessioun,
Sith folk ne doon hir operacioun
Alwey, as dooth the fyr, lo, in his kinde.
For, God it woot, men may wel often finde
A lordes sone do shame and vileynie;
And he that wole han pris of his gentrie,
For he was boren of a gentil hous,
And hadde his eldres noble and vertuous,
And nel himselven do no gentil dedis,
Ne folwen his gentil auncestre that deed is,
He nis nat gentil, be he duc or erl;
For vileyns sinful dedes make a cherl.
Thy gentillesse nis but renomee
Of thine auncestres, for hire heigh bountee,
Which is a strange thing to thy persone.
For gentillesse cometh fro God allone.
Thanne comth oure verray gentillesse of grace;
It was no thing biquethe us with oure place.
　Thenketh hou noble, as seith Valerius,
Was thilke Tullius Hostillius,
That out of poverte roos to heigh noblesse.
Reedeth Senek, and redeth eek Boece;
Ther shul ye seen expres that it no drede is
That he is gentil that dooth gentil dedis.
And therfore, leeve housbonde, I thus conclude:
Al were it that mine auncestres were rude,
Yet may the hye God, and so hope I,

1150

1160

1170

Grante me grace to liven vertuously.
Thanne am I gentil, whan that I biginne
To liven vertuously and weive sinne.
  And ther as ye of poverte me repreeve,
The hye God, on whom that we bileeve,
In wilful poverte chees to live his lyf.
And certes every man, maiden, or wyf,   1180
May understonde that Jhesus, hevene king,
Ne wolde nat chese a vicious living.
Glad poverte is an honest thing, certeyn;
This wole Senec and othere clerkes seyn.
Whoso that halt him paid of his poverte,
I holde him riche, al hadde he nat a sherte.
He that coveiteth is a povre wight,
For he wolde han that is nat in his might;
But he that noght hath, ne coveiteth have,
Is riche, although ye holde him but a knave.   1190
Verray poverte, it singeth proprely;
Juvenal seith of poverte mirily:
"The povre man, whan he goth by the weye,
Bifore the theves he may singe and pleye."
Poverte is hateful good and, as I gesse,
A ful greet bringere-out of bisinesse;
A greet amendere eek of sapience
To him that taketh it in pacience.
Poverte is this, although it seme alenge,
Possessioun that no wight wol chalenge.   1200
Poverte ful ofte, whan a man is lowe,
Maketh his God and eek himself to knowe.
Poverte a spectacle is, as thinketh me,
Thurgh which he may his verray freendes see.
And therfore, sire, sin that I noght yow greve,

73

Of my poverte namoore ye me repreve.
   Now, sire, of elde ye repreve me;
And certes, sire, thogh noon auctoritee
Were in no book, ye gentils of honour
1210   Seyn that men sholde an oold wight doon favour,
And clepe him fader, for youre gentillesse;
And auctours shal I finden, as I gesse.
   Now ther ye seye that I am foul and old,
Than drede you noght to been a cokewold;
For filthe and eelde, also moot I thee,
Been grete wardeyns upon chastitee.
But nathelees, sin I knowe youre delit,
I shal fulfille youre worldly appetit.
   Chese now,' quod she, 'oon of thise thinges tweye:
1220   To han me foul and old til that I deye,
And be to yow a trewe, humble wyf,
And nevere yow displese in al my lyf;
Or elles ye wol han me yong and fair,
And take youre aventure of the repair
That shal be to youre hous by cause of me,
Or in som oother place, may wel be.
Now chese yourselven, wheither that yow liketh.'
   This knight aviseth him and sore siketh,
But atte laste he seyde in this manere:
1230   'My lady and my love, and wyf so deere,
I put me in youre wise governance;
Cheseth youreself which may be moost plesance,
And moost honour to yow and me also.
I do no fors the wheither of the two;
For as yow liketh, it suffiseth me.'
   'Thanne have I gete of yow maistrie,' quod she,
'Sin I may chese and governe as me lest?'

'Ye, certes, wyf,' quod he, 'I holde it best.'
'Kis me,' quod she, 'we be no lenger wrothe;
For, by my trouthe, I wol be to yow bothe,   1240
This is to seyn, ye, bothe fair and good.
I prey to God that I moote sterven wood,
But I to yow be also good and trewe
As evere was wyf, sin that the world was newe.
And but I be to-morn as fair to seene
As any lady, emperice, or queene,
That is bitwixe the est and eke the west,
Dooth with my lyf and deth right as yow lest.
Cast up the curtin, looke how that it is.'
    And whan the knight saugh verraily al this,   1250
That she so fair was, and so yong therto,
For joye he hente hire in his armes two,
His herte bathed in a bath of blisse.
A thousand time a-rewe he gan hire kisse,
And she obeyed him in every thing
That mighte doon him plesance or liking.
    And thus they live unto hir lives ende
In parfit joye; and Jhesu Crist us sende
Housbondes meeke, yonge, and fressh abedde,
And grace t'overbide hem that we wedde;   1260
And eek I praye Jhesu shorte hir lives
That wol nat be governed by hir wives;
And olde and angry nigardes of dispence,
God sende hem soone verray pestilence!

NOTES

The notes incorporate the following abbreviations:

Boece   *De Consolatione Philosophiae* of Boethius, translated by
          Chaucer
GP   *The General Prologue*, ed. James Winny. Cambridge,
          1965
ME   Middle English
OE   Old English
OED   *The Oxford English Dictionary*. Oxford, 1961
RR   *Le Roman de la Rose*, ed. M. Méon. Paris, 1814
Skeat   *The Complete Works of Geoffrey Chaucer*, ed. W. W.
          Skeat. 2nd ed. Oxford, 1963
Wyclif   Wyclifite translation of the New Testament (*c.* 1380),
          ed. Forshall and Maddon. Oxford, 1879

1. *experience* Compare the remark of La Vieille in *RR*,
13007–9:

> Mès ge sai tout par la pratique
> Experiment m'en ont fait sage
> Que j'ai hanté tout mon aâge.

1–2. *though noon auctoritee were in this world* 'even if no
textual authority could be cited'. Such *auctoritee* is provided
by 1 Corinthians vii. 28: 'If thou hast taken a wif, thou hast
not sinned...nethelesse siche schulen [such persons shall]
have tribulacioun of fleisch' (Wyclif).

4. *twelve yeer* This admission of early marriage seems to conflict with the reference to 'oother compaignye in youthe'
(*GP*, 463).

6. *at chirche dore* Only persons of high rank were married
inside the church. The ceremony at the door of the church was
followed by nuptial mass before the altar.

7. *if I so ofte mighte have ywedded be* 'if a person can properly
be said to have been married so many times'. The canonists of
the medieval Church contested the legality of second marriages.

8. *worthy men in hir degree* 'decent, well-to-do citizens'. The
Wife herself has been 'a worthy womman al hir live' (*GP*,
461).

9. *me was toold* 'it was told to me'.

11. *the Cane* 'Cana'; see John ii. 1.
13. *ne sholde wedded be but ones* 'should marry only once'.
14. *which a sharp word* 'what a pointed retort'.
    for the nones 'immediately, on the spur of the moment'.
16. *the Samaritan* See John iv. 6 ff.
18. *that now hath thee* 'with whom you are living now'.
20. *I kan nat seyn* The Wife is borrowing Chaucer's innocence.
23. *how manye mighte she have in mariage* According to medieval canon law, a woman was permitted to marry only once, and any subsequent marriage was to be regarded as bigamous. The Wife demands rebelliously what biblical authority can be quoted in support of this judgement.
24-5. *Yet herde I nevere...diffinicioun* 'In all my life I never yet heard it firmly stated what the proper number of husbands was'.
28. *God bad us* See Genesis i. 28.
30. *he seyde* Christ; see Matthew xix. 5.
32. *of no nombre mencion made he* 'he said nothing about a permitted number of husbands'.
33. *bigamie* In the canonists' sense, of marrying a second time.
    octogamie 'marrying eight times'. The term appears in Jerome's *Epistola adversus Jovinianum*, which supplied many of the ideas repeated by the Wife. See especially line 675 below, where she refers explicitly to this 'book again Jovinian'.
35. *lo, heere* Literally, 'look, listen'; a colloquial phrase with the sense of 'then what about...?'; 'lo' was commonly used in citing an authority.
36. *wives mo than oon* 'more than one wife'. According to 1 Kings xi. 3, Solomon had seven hundred wives and three hundred concubines.
37. *as wolde God it were leveful unto me* 'would to God it were allowed to me'.
39. *which yifte* 'what a gift!'.
39-40. The rhyme *wives, alive is* shows how the plural ending *-es* was pronounced as a separate syllable.
41. *as to my wit* 'as I think'.
43. *so wel was him on live* 'such a blessed life he enjoyed'. The dative phrase 'on live' corresponds to 'alive' in modern English.
45. *whan that evere he shal* 'whenever he happens to arrive'.

46. *I wol nat kepe me chaast in al* 'I don't at all wish to remain unmarried'.

49. *th'apostle* St Paul. See 1 Corinthians vii. 9: 'But I seye to hem that ben not weddid, and to widewis, it is good to hem if thei dwellen so as I' (Wyclif).

50. *a Goddes half* 'in God's name'.
    where it liketh me 'wherever it please me'.

52. *bet is to be wedded than to brinne* 'Better marry than burn' (1 Corinthians vii).

53. *what rekketh me* 'what does it matter to me?'.
    seye vileynie 'are scandalized by'.

54. *Lameth* See Genesis iv. 19–23. He is described in *The Squire's Tale*, 550–1, as the man 'that alderfirst bigan to loven two'. Skeat quotes a comment by Bell about the confusion running through this discussion between marrying twice and having two wives at once.

59. *in any manere age* 'at any time in history'.

63. *it is no drede* 'there are no two ways about it'.

65. *he seyde that precept therof hadde he noon* Referring to 1 Corinthians vii. 6, where St Paul gives advice without claiming any divine authority for his statement: 'But I seie this thing as giving leeve, not bi commaundement' (Wyclif).

66. *to been oon* 'to remain single'.

67. *conseilling is no comandement* 'advising isn't ordering'.

70. *with the dede* 'by that act', 'by doing so'.

73. *Poul* St Paul.
    atte leeste 'at all events'.

74. *his maister* Christ.

75. *the dart is set up for virginitee* Evidently the Wife is thinking of the prize in the race referred to by St Paul in 1 Corinthians ix. 24, to be won by those who deny themselves marriage.

76. *cacche whoso may, who renneth best lat see* 'catch that catch may [i.e. let everyone do his best], we'll see who runs fastest'. 'So renne ye, that ye catche' (Wyclif).

78. *but ther as God lust give it of his might* 'only where God is pleased to bestow it through his divine power'.

79. *th'apostel was a maide* St Paul was unmarried.

81. *he wolde that every wight were swich as he* 'he wished everyone to be like himself in this respect': referring to 1 Corinthians vii. 7: 'For I wolde that alle men be as my silf' (Wyclif).

82. *al nis but conseil* 'it's nothing more than advice'.

83. *for to been* 'to be'.

84. *leve of indulgence* Referring to the allowance given by
St Paul to those who found the life of chastity too difficult:
'That if thei conteynen not hem silf, be thei weddid' (Wyclif).
so nis it no repreve 'it is not a matter for reproach'. Middle
English allowed such use of the double negative for emphasis.
Compare: line 98, 'I nil nat'; line 100, 'he nath nat'; and
line 148, 'I nam nat precius'.

85. *to wedde me, if that my make die* 'to marry, if my husband
dies'. *Wedde me* is reflexive, not transitive.

86. *withouten excepcion of bigamie* 'without being accused of
bigamy', in the canonists' sense of the term.

87. *al were it good* 'although it would be laudable'; still
following St Paul, here in 1 Corinthians vii. 1: 'It is good to a
man to touche not a womman' (Wyclif).

89. *peril is bothe fyr and tow t'assemble* 'it's dangerous to bring
fire and flax together'.

90. *what this ensample may resemble* 'what this proverb
signifies'.

92. *wedding in freletee* 'marrying from inability to resist the
sexual urge': see line 84 above, and note.

93-4. *freletee clepe I...chastitee* 'I must call it weakness,
except in cases where husband and wife wish to live together
without sexual relations'; as St Paul recommends in 1
Corinthians vii. 5.

95. *I graunte it wel* 'I'm perfectly happy about this'.

96. *thogh maidenhede preferre bigamie* 'even if continence be
morally preferable to marrying twice'.

97. *it liketh hem* 'it pleases them' (i.e. the people mentioned
in lines 93-4 above).

100. *he nath nat every vessel al of gold* 'not every piece of his
table-ware is made of gold'.

101. *and doon hir lord servise* 'and still serve their owner's
needs'. The Wife is quoting from 2 Timothy ii. 20: 'In a
greet hous ben not oneli vessels of gold and silver, but also of
tree and of erthe' (Wyclif).

103. *a propre yifte* 'some special gift or talent of his own'. The
Wife has now moved to 1 Corinthians vii. 7: 'But eche man hath
his propre yifte of God; oon thus, and another thus' (Wyclif).

104. *as him liketh shifte* 'as it pleases him to distribute them'.

106. *and continence eek with devocion* 'and so is continence,
when undertaken for spiritual reasons'.

107. *that of perfeccion is welle* 'who is the fountain-head of moral perfection'.

108. *bad nat every wight* This evasion of the precept set out in Matthew xix. 21 is also made by Faux-Semblant, in *RR*, 11568 ff.:

> Et sachiés, là où Diex commande
> Qui li prodons quanqu'il a vende,
> Et doint as povres et le sive,
> Por ce ne vuet-il pas qu'il vive
> De li servir en mendience:
> Ce ne fu onques sa sentence;
> Ains entent que de ses mains euvre,
> Et qu'il le sive par bonne euvre.

110. *his foore* 'his footsteps, example'.

113. *bistowe the flour of al myn age* 'spend my mature energy and attraction'.

114. *fruit of mariage* Not meaning children, in whom the Wife shows no interest, but sexual fulfilment. Like Chauntecleer, she makes love 'moore for delit than world to multiplie'. Fruit is something to be plucked and eaten.

115–16. *to what conclusion were membres maad of generacion?* 'for what purpose were reproductive organs made?'.

117. *and of so parfit wys a wight ywroght* *Wight* usually means 'person', as in line 77 above. Here it has the less common meaning of 'a little thing'. The Wife is admiring the formation of the sexual organs—the 'thinges smale' of line 121 below.

118. *trusteth right wel* 'believe you me': using the polite imperative form.

119. *glose whoso wole, and seye bothe up and doun* 'whoever likes to explain it, and whatever arguments they bring forward'. Cf. line 26; the Wife enjoys a gibe at ingenious theologians who cast about, somewhat desperately, for elaborate and bad reasons for denying nature.

121. *oure bothe thinges smale* 'the organs which both men and women possess'.

122. *to knowe a femele from a male* 'to distinguish between male and female'.

124. *the experience woot wel it is noght so* Experience—the keyword of the Wife's argument—proves that this is not the case. Another triumphant line, like 112.

125. *so that* 'provided'.

126. *maked ben* 'are made': cf. 'dronken ben', line 852 below.

127–8. *for office, and for ese of engendrure* 'for emptying the bladder, and for sexual pleasure'.

128. *ther we nat God displese* 'in which we do not offend God'.

130. *hire dette* See 1 Corinthians vii. 3: 'The hosebonde yelde dette to the wiif, and also the wiif to the hosebonde' (Wyclif). The point is made again in *The Parson's Tale*, where the speaker—following Wyclif closely—affirms that man and wife should 'yelden everich of hem to oother the dette of hire bodies; for neither of hem hath power of his owene body'. The Wife returns to this point in lines 152–61 below, but without recognizing a mutual obligation upon both partners.

132. *his sely instrument* Sely or *seely* is the ME predecessor of modern 'silly', which embodies changes of sense and spelling. By describing the penis as a *sely instrument* the Wife means that it is a simple tool; but as the term also meant 'happy, blessed', she is expressing approval as well. Since *sely* had the further meaning of 'morally good or innocent', the Wife may also be rejecting the notion that the sexual parts are corrupting and shameful. She is later to express considerable pride in her own sexual attributes: see especially line 608 below.

133. *maad upon a creature* 'fashioned as part of the human body'.

138. *take of chastitee no cure* 'consider virginity unimportant'.

139. *shapen as a man* 'having a man's body and physical nature'.

143–4. *Lat hem...lat us...* 'If they are...then we can be called...'.

breed of pured whete-seed 'bread made from refined wheat-flour'.

145. *Mark telle kan* Not St Mark but St John speaks of barley loaves in his account of the miracle: see John vi. 9.

146. *refresshed* Cf. line 38. The Wife's tacit analogy between barley-bread and sexual enjoyment is impudently strengthened by her use of the same term in both allusions.

148. *I nam nat precius* 'I'm not genteel and fastidious'.

151. *if I be daungerous* 'if I show any reluctance or unwillingness'.

153. *whan that him list* 'whenever it pleases him to'.

paye his dette An activity which the Wife is prepared to interpret in the most literal sense: see lines 409–12 below.

154. *I wol nat lette* 'I will not be thwarted'.

156-7. *and have his tribulacion withal upon his flessh* Her husband must suffer the 'wo that is in mariage' of which St Paul warns, and to which she has referred in her opening remark.

159. *and noght he* The Wife is wilfully mistaken. The husband is to enjoy the same conjugal rights as his wife: see 1 Corinthians vii. 4: 'The womman hath not power of hir bodi, but the hosebonde; and the hosebonde hath not power of his bodi, but the womman' (Wyclif).

161. *and bad oure housebondes for to love us weel* See Ephesians v. 25: 'Men, love ye youre wives' (Wyclif). The Wife conveniently ignores the admonition three verses later, exhorting wives to love their husbands.

162. *al this sentence me liketh every deel* 'this pronouncement is very much to my liking'.

165. *in this cas* 'on this subject'.

166. *I was aboute to wedde a wyf* Both *GP*, 691-3, and *The Pardoner's Tale*, 666-9, show the Pardoner to be a natural eunuch. His remark here seems a boast designed to conceal this humiliating defect.

167. *what sholde I bye it on my flessh so deere?* 'why should I bring misery upon myself at such a high price?'. The use of *what* in the sense of 'why' is common in Chaucer: cf. line 213 below, and *GP*, 184.

168. *no wyf to-yeere* 'no wife this year'; or possibly, never.

170. *thou shalt drinken of another tonne* 'your next drink will come from a different barrel'. This sounds like a proverbial expression; but the Wife could be referring to the draught of 'moiste and corny ale' which the Pardoner drinks before embarking on his story: see *Introduction to the Pardoner's Tale*, 29.

171. *er that I go* 'before I've done'.

172. *my tale* Here and at lines 186 and 193 below the tale is the Wife's reminiscences, not her formal story.

174. *expert in al myn age* 'having a lifelong experience'.

178. *er thou to ny approche* 'before you get too close'.

179. *ensamples mo than ten* 'more than ten illustrations'; more than a few.

180-1. *whoso that nil...corrected be* 'the man who disregards cautionary examples will himself become one'.

182. *Ptholomee* Ptolemy, astronomer and geographer of the ancient world.

183. *Almageste* Ptolemy's treatise on astronomy, whose familiar Greek title was μεγιστη or greatest (work). The book came to medieval scholars by way of the Arabs, by whom it had been preserved during the Dark Ages and known as 'al majisti'. This half-Arabic title was then taken over by its European readers. The proverbial saying quoted by the Wife does not appear in the Almageste, but was ascribed to Ptolemy by other writers.

   take it there 'learn it from there'.

184. *Dame* 'madam'. The Wife is not entitled to this form of address; but no doubt she shares the opinion of the Gildsmen's wives, that 'it is ful fair to been ycleped "madame"' (*GP*, 378). See also *The Reeve's Tale*, line 36.

   if youre wil it were 'if you would be so kind'. It is usually the Host who encourages or exhorts a speaker to get on with his tale. The Pardoner is showing some inclination to usurp the Host's authority.

186. *spareth for no man* 'hold back nothing, whoever objects'.

187. *us yonge men* The Pardoner attempts to disguise his lack of vitality by dressing and behaving like a dashing young man: see *GP*, 682–5. Now he claims to be one.

188. *sith it may yow like* 'since it may please you'; or perhaps— ironically—'since you think you'll enjoy it'.

190. *after my fantasie* 'according to my inclination or whim'. In a poet, *fantasie* was the faculty of imagination. Chaucer may be speaking under cover of the Wife's apology.

191. *as taketh not agrief of that I seye* 'don't take offence from what I relate': *as* being used to introduce an imperative verb.

192. *nat but for to pleye* 'simply to entertain'.

193. The Wife is not diverted from her stream of reminiscence and moralizing for another 650 lines.

194. *as evere moote I* 'as ever may I'; meaning 'May I be denied such pleasure if this is not true'.

196. *as thre of hem* 'of whom three'.

198. *the statut holde* 'carry out the obligation set down by St Paul': see line 130 above, and note.

200. *what I meene of this* 'what I mean by this'—that her old husbands were virtually impotent.

201. *as help me* 'so help me'.

202. *swinke* 'sweating labour', here in bed.

203. *I tolde of it no stoor* 'I cared nothing for their distress'.

205. *me neded nat do lenger diligence* 'there was no further need for me to exert myself'.

206. *doon hem reverence* 'treat them respectfully'.

208. *I ne tolde no deyntee of hir love* 'I set no value on their love'.

209. *wol bisie hire evere in oon* 'will busy herself continuously'.

210. *ther as she hath noon* 'so long as she has none'.

211. *hoolly in myn hond* 'completely under my thumb'.

213. *what sholde I taken keep* 'why should I trouble myself'?.

214. *but it were* 'except for'.

217–18. *the bacon... in Essex at Dunmowe* The Dunmow Flitch; a side of bacon annually awarded to the married couple who had not quarrelled or wished themselves single during the previous year.

219. *after my lawe* 'according to my custom'.

223. *God it woot* 'God knows'.

224. *herkneth hou I baar me proprely* 'let me tell you how well I managed things'.

225. *ye wise wives* The only women in the Wife's audience are the Prioress and her attendant Nun. Chaucer seems to imagine her addressing a wider circle of listeners, such as his poems might have found at court and who form the real audience of his tales.

226. *bere hem wrong on honde* 'delude them'.

227. *kan ther no man* 'no man knows how to'.

229. *by wives* 'with respect to wives'.

230. *but if it be whan they hem misavise* 'except on those occasions when they disregard their own interests'.

231. *if that she kan hir good* 'if she recognizes where her private interests lie'.

232. *bere him on honde that the cow is wood* 'delude him into believing that the chough is mad'. The Wife is referring to the folk-story of the tell-tale bird, of which a version is related by the Manciple later in the pilgrimage. A married woman entertains her lover in sight of the talking bird, who tells the husband on his return that he is a cuckold. The wife denies the charge, and asserts that the bird is mad. To prove her point, she and her maid simulate a thunderstorm over the bird's cage the following night. The next morning, the bird speaks of having been kept awake by the rough weather, and the husband is persuaded that the bird is out of its wits.

234. *of hir assent* 'the maid consenting to the deception'.

235. *is this thyn array?* 'is this how you carry on?'.

237. *over al ther she gooth* 'wherever she goes'.

238. *I have no thrifty clooth* 'I haven't a decent thing to wear'.

242. *lat thy japes be!* 'give over these tricks!'.

244. *withouten gilt* 'in all innocence'.

245. *pleye unto his hous* 'take a stroll in the direction of his house'.

246. *dronken as a mous* This expression also appears in *The Knight's Tale*, line 403. Its earlier form was 'drunk as a drowned mouse'.

247. *on thy bench* The common form of domestic seat. Chairs were provided only for persons of special dignity: hence the term 'chairman'.

   with ivel preef! 'misfortune take you!'.

249. *for costage* 'because of the expense involved'. A poor woman brought no dowry.

250. *of heigh parage* 'of high rank or birth'.

252. *malencolie* 'attacks of sulkiness, dumps'.

254. *every holour wol hire have* 'every lecher wants her'.

255. *she may no while in chastitee abide* 'she can't remain a decent woman long'.

256. *upon ech a side* 'on every side'.

257. *for richesse* 'for our money'.

258. *for oure shap* The Wife may be referring generally to her figure, or specifically to the genitalia: see *OED* 'shape', 16.

259. *for she kan outher singe or daunce* 'because she is an accomplished dancer or singer'. The stronger sense of *kan*, meaning 'to know how', is being employed.

260. *gentillesse and daliaunce* 'delicate manners and playfulness in love'. Both terms involve several shades of meaning.

261. *hir handes and hir armes smale* Slender hands and arms seem to have been considered a special attraction of medieval women: see, for another example, *Troilus and Criseyde*, iii, 1247.

262. *by thy tale* 'according to your story'.

263. *may nat kepe a castel wal* 'cannot hold a castle wall against attack'.

264. *it may so longe assailled been over al* 'it is open to assault everywhere the whole time'.

265. *if that she be foul* 'should she be ugly'.

266. *that she may se* 'whom she sets eyes on'.

Notes

268. *hire to chepe* 'to do business with her'. The Wife returns to this commercial image at line 521 below.

269. *ne noon so grey goos* 'there's no goose so grey'. The expression is proverbial, and means that each of us has a potential partner somewhere in the land.

270. *wol been withoute make* 'wishes to be without a mate'.

272. *that no man wole, his thankes, helde* 'which nobody would willingly keep'. The genitive form *thankes*, literally 'of thought', or 'of good will', was used adverbially with the sense of 'willingly', as in the present instance.

275. *that entendeth unto hevene* 'who has his mind fixed on heaven'.

277. *moote thy welked nekke be tobroke!* 'may your withered neck be broken!'.

278–9. *dropping houses, ... smoke, and chiding wives* The expression is proverbial; compare *Melibee*, 1085: 'Thre thinges driven a man out of his hous, that is to seyn, smoke, dropping [dripping] of reyn, and wikked wives'.

281. *what eyleth swich an old man for to chide?* 'what could be the matter with an old man, to make him scold like this?'.

283. *til we be fast* 'until we have made ourselves secure, by marrying'.

284. *wel may that be* 'most certainly this is'.

285. *hors* 'horses': cf. *GP*, 74, 'his hors were goode'.

287–9. *Bacins, lavours*, etc. All these nouns are subject of 'been assayed' in line 286. All these things are tried out before purchase.

290. *folk of wives maken noon assay* 'people make no trial of the women they intend to marry'.

294. *but if that thou wolt* 'unless you do'; 'if you don't'.

298. *make me fressh and gay* 'make me feel young and lively'.

299, 300. *norice, chamberere* The Wife has already referred to her maid at line 241 above. It seems doubtful whether a woman of her social station would retain three domestic servants. But much of the Wife's argument from line 235 to line 315 is adopted from St Jerome, sometimes without complete regard for the different domestic background of Chaucer's tale. A nurse, a nursemaid and a handsome secretary all appear in the household described in St Jerome's quotation from Theophrastus: see Appendix 2, p. 123.

303. *oure apprentice Janekin* Described as 'our clerke' at line 595 below, where he is about to become her fifth husband.
   and yet 'and again'.

86

304. *for his crispe heer* 'because of his curly hair'. The Wife lets
her admiration and desire appear, despite her denial.

305. *squiereth me bothe up and doun* 'escorts me everywhere'.

307. *I wol him noght* 'I don't want him at all'.

308. *with sorwe* 'plague take you!'.

311. *wenestow make an idiot?* 'do you think to have me treated
as insane, with no rights to my own property?'.

    oure dame 'the lady of the house'; herself. The possessive
adjective is used again in lines 432, 713 and 793 below. It has
the sense of close association rather than of personal possession.
In some districts of England, children commonly speak of
'our Mum', meaning 'my mother', and of 'our Bill', meaning
'my brother Bill'.

312. *Seint Jame* St James, whose famous shrine at Compostella,
in Spain, the Wife had visited as a pilgrim: see *GP*, 468.

315. *that oon thou shalt forgo* 'you're going to lose one of them'.
    maugree thine yen 'for all your watchfulness' (literally:
'despite your eyes').

319. *I wol nat leve no talis* 'I shan't allow gossip to be repeated
to me'.

320. *Alis* Alice, but Alison at line 804 below.

321. *taketh kep or charge* 'exercises careful watch over'.

322. *we wol ben at oure large* 'we like to enjoy complete liberty'.

323–36. The Wife slips into a half-justification of her suspected
adultery.

324–5. *Ptholome...his Almageste* See lines 182–3 above, and
note. Skeat observes: 'We need not search our Ptolemy for
this saying'.

327. *that rekketh nevere who hath the world in honde* 'the
wisest man is the contented one, who doesn't care how much
another man's wealth exceeds his'.

329. *have thou ynogh* 'so long as you have all you want'.
    what thar thee 'why should you?'.

332. *ye shul have queynte right ynogh at eve* 'you'll have all the
sex you want at night'. Even if the Wife has been satisfying
her lover during the day, there will be plenty left for her
husband: see line 335 below. Although the straightforward
term *queynte* was presumably less shocking to polite ears than
its modern derivative would be, the word could never have
been in general use. The Wife is more delicately allusive at
line 608 below.

333. *to greet a nigard* 'a terrible miser'.

335. *never the lasse light* 'not a whit less light'.
336. *thee thar nat pleyne thee* 'you haven't any call for complaint'.
339. *peril of oure chastitee* 'endangering our chastity'.
340. *with sorwe!* 'devil take you!'.
    thou most enforce thee 'you have to rub the point in'.
341. *the Apostles* St Timothy's. The reference is to 1 Timothy
    ii. 9: 'With schamefastnesse and sobrenesse araiynge hem
    silf, not in writhun heeris, ethir in gold, ethir peerlis, ethir
    preciouse cloth' (Wyclif).
346–7. *After thy text, ne after thy rubriche, I wol nat wirche as
    muchel as a gnat* 'I won't give a fly for your quoted authority,
    nor for your interpretation of it'.
350. *wel dwellen in his in* 'stay at home all day, without going
    out'.
353. *er any day be dawed* 'long before daybreak'.
354. *goon a-caterwawed* 'go caterwauling', or looking for a
    mate.
356. *my borel for to shewe Borel*, or *burel*, is coarse woollen cloth
    or clothing. But if the Wife is *gay* (previous line), she would
    not be wearing such material. Either she is speaking sarcastic-
    ally, or using *borel* as a euphemism.
358. *Argus* A figure of Greek mythology, possessing a hundred
    eyes.
359. *as he kan best* 'as he best knows how'.
360. *but me lest* 'unless it please me'. *Lest* is the Kentish form
    of *list*, and suggests Chaucer's own form of speech rather than
    the Wife of Bath's. This regional form appears again at line
    854 below.
361. *make his berd* 'outwit or delude him'.
    so moot I thee! 'so may I prosper!'; meaning 'so help me if
    I wouldn't!'.
364. *no wight may endure the ferthe* 'nobody can tolerate the fourth
    thing'. 'For three things the earth is disquieted, and for four
    which it cannot bear' (Proverbs xxx. 21).
368. *been ther none othere maner resemblances?* 'is there no other
    sort of comparison?'.
370. *but if a sely wyf be oon of tho?* 'but a poor innocent wife
    must be one of them?'.
372. *ther water may nat dwelle* 'where water quickly disappears'—
    as in a desert.
373. *wilde fyr* 'wild fire'; a combination of highly inflammable
    materials used in warfare.

375. *that brent wole be* 'that can be burnt'.
376. *right as wormes shende a tree* 'just as insects destroy a tree'.
380. *baar I stifly...on honde* 'boldly I deluded'.
381. *in hir dronkenesse* 'when they were drunk'.
382. *I took witnesse* 'I called as witness'.
383. *my nece* Another member of the household, mentioned again at line 537 below. Jankin has now become the Wife's accomplice.
385. *ful giltelees* 'although they were completely innocent'.
386. *bite and whine* 'both bite (when in a bad temper) and whine or whinny as if wanting a caress (when in a good one)' (Skeat).
387. *and yit was in the gilt* 'and yet was myself in the wrong'.
388. *often time hadde I been spilt* 'several times I should have been ruined'.
389. *whoso that first to mille comth, first grint* 'first come, first served'. The Wife forestalls just accusation by making her own false charge against her husband before he can utter his complaint.
390. *so was oure werre ystint* 'so domestic strife was prevented'.
391. *ful glade to excuse hem blive* 'very glad to exonerate themselves quickly'.
392. *they nevere agilte hir live* 'they had never been guilty in their lives'.
393. *of wenches wolde I beren hem on honde* 'I would pretend to believe that they kept mistresses'.
394. *for sik unnethes mighte they stonde* 'they were almost too ill to stand on their feet'.
395. *his herte* From speaking of her old husbands collectively, the Wife now discusses one in particular.
396. *wende that I hadde of him so greet chiertee* 'supposed that I loved him so possessively'.
399. *under that colour hadde I many a mirthe* 'this pretence provided me with many a laugh'.
400. *al swich wit* 'all such cunning and ingenuity'.
    in oure birthe 'at birth'.
401-2. *God hath yive to wommen kindely* 'God has assigned to women as part of their nature'.
404. *the bettre in ech degree* 'the upper hand in every way'.
406. *as by* 'for instance, by'.
407. *hadden they meschaunce* 'they had a miserable time'.
408. *do hem no plesaunce* 'give them no enjoyment'.

412. *suffre him do his nicetee* 'allow him to satisfy his desire'. The commonest meaning of *nice* in ME was 'foolish, stupid'. *Nicetee* is used in the sense of 'lust', but here the term takes some of the sense of the adjective, and implies 'a silly business'. The Wife is mocking her old husbands' attempts to make love.

414. *winne whoso may* 'make profit where you can'.
    al is for to selle 'everything has its price'.

415. *none haukes lure* Hawks do not return to the falconer unless offered a lure.

416. *for winning* 'in order to make money'.

417. *make me a feyned appetit* 'pretend to be sexually excited'.

418. *bacon* 'old meat'; meaning her old husbands.
    delit 'sexual gratification'.

419. *that made me that evere I wolde hem chide* 'it was for this reason—the distaste I felt for them sexually—that I was forever nagging them'. The Wife analyses herself with some acuteness.

422. *I quitte hem word for word* 'I paid them back in the same currency'.

424. *though I right now sholde make my testament* 'if I were now to make my will'; in which the Wife would settle her outstanding debts and obligations.

425. *that it nis quit* 'which hasn't been repaid'.

426. *by my wit* 'by cunning'.

427. *yeve it up, as for the beste* 'wisely give up the struggle'.

428. *in reste* 'at peace'.

430. *faille of his conclusion* 'fall short of his hopes'; 'not get his way'.

431. *goode lief* 'beloved', 'darling'.

432. *Wilkin, oure sheep* Meaning that her husband should be equally docile. The sheep appears to be a ram. The name 'wilkin' was later given to a ramming instrument.

433. *lat me ba* Addressing him as a refractory child being given 'kissums' in token of forgiveness.

435. *a sweete spiced conscience* 'a scrupulous sense of doing right'. The same phrase is used in *GP*, 528, without sarcasm.

436. *Jobes* 'Job's'.

437. *suffreth alwey* 'go on enduring affliction'.

438. *but ye do* 'unless you do'.

439. *it is fair to have a wyf in pees* 'it's a fine thing to live peaceably with your wife'.

440. *moste bowen, doutelees* 'must give way to the other, for sure'.

441–2. *sith a man is moore resonable than womman is* 'since men are more sensible creatures than women'. The ingenuity of the argument disproves the Wife's contention.

442. *ye moste been suffrable* 'you must endure it patiently'.

444. *is it for ye wolde have my queynte allone?* 'is it because you want to keep my body to yourself exclusively?'.

446. *Peter!* 'by St Peter!'.

447. *my bele chose* 'my nice thing': again at line 510 below. The term is evidently a courtly euphemism adapted from the current expression *privy chose*. It contrasts sharply with the strong vernacular term used at lines 332 and 444 above. The Wife is saying that if she had been a prostitute she would be richly dressed. Yet lines 411–18 show that she did sell herself.

448. *as fressh as is a rose* 'like a fine lady': but for overtones of *fressh* compare lines 38 and 298 above.

449. *for youre owene tooth* 'for your private enjoyment alone'.

450. *ye be to blame* A scolding phrase, here used roguishly: 'What a terrible man you are!'.

451. *hadde we on honde* 'passed between us'.

455. *ful of ragerie* 'brimful of passion and vitality'. Cf. *The Merchant's Tale*, lines 634–5:

> He was al coltissh, ful of ragerie,
> And ful of jargon as a flekked pie.

456. *joly as a pie* 'as merry and talkative as a magpie'.

457. *an harpe smale* Such as the Friar plays: see *GP*, 268.

460. *Metellius* The story is related by the Roman historian Valerius Maximus, of whom the Wife evidently learned from her fifth husband. The anecdotes concerning Simplicius Gallus and 'another Romain', brought in at lines 642 and 647 below, come from the same chapter of Valerius's work, a long handbook on rhetoric illustrated by anecdotes of all kinds.

461. *birafte his wyf hir lyf* 'murdered his wife': literally, 'deprived his wife [of] her life'. The same construction appears at line 475 below.

462. *for she drank wyn* 'for drinking wine'.

464. *on Venus moste I thinke* 'I can't help thinking about making love'.

466. *a likerous mouth moste han a likerous tail* The expression is proverbial: compare *The Pardoner's Tale*, line 198, 'luxurie [lechery] is in wyn and dronkenesse'. The Wife uses *tail* in its sexual sense: cf. *The Shipman's Tale*, line 434.

467. *in wommen vinolent is no defence* 'tipsy women can't protect themselves against seduction'.

469. *whan that it remembreth me* 'when it comes back to me'. The construction *remember upon* is also used in *The Nun's Priest's Tale*, line 267. The whole of this passage shows Chaucer following *RR* very closely:

> Par diex! si me plest-il encores:
> Quant ge m'i sui bien porpensée,
> Moult me délite en ma pensée,
> Et me resbaudissent li membre
> Quant de mon bon tens me remembre,
> Et de la jolivete vie
> Dont mes cuers a si grant envie.   (13136–42)

470. *my jolitee* 'gaiety and vivacity', with overtones of sexual eagerness. The Pardoner attempts to simulate this manner: see *GP*, 682.

473. *as in my time* 'in my day'.

474. *that al wole envenime* 'that likes to destroy everything'.

475. *hath me biraft* 'has stolen from me'.

476. *lat go!* 'let it go!'.

477. *namoore to telle* 'nothing more to set store by'.

480. *now wol I tellen* Repeating the still unfulfilled promise made at line 452 above.

481. *I seye* 'as I was saying': at lines 453 ff.

482. *that he of any oother had delit* 'that he should find his pleasure in some other woman'. As at line 418 above, *delit* implies sexual gratification.

483. *Seint Joce* Judocus, a Breton saint. Chaucer probably borrowed the reference from the *Testament* of Jean de Meun, one of the authors of the *Roman de la Rose*; but the Wife could be supposed to have encountered St Judocus during her continental pilgrimages.

484. *I made him of the same wode a croce* Another proverbial expression. The Wife repaid her husband by making him as angry and jealous as herself.

485. *nat of my body* 'not by committing adultery'.

486. *I made folk swich cheere* 'I behaved to other people in such a charming manner'.

487. *in his owene grece I made him frie* Proverbial: compare the modern saying, 'to stew in his own juice'.

489. *in erthe I was his purgatorie* 'I made purgatory for him on earth'; a sardonic joke with many medieval parallels. One antifeminist writer makes God defend the institution of matrimony as a form of purgatory on earth, by which the sinful are saved from damnation hereafter.

490. *his soule be in glorie* 'in heaven', which even the souls of the blessed could not reach without first passing through purgatory.

492. *his shoo ful bitterly him wrong* 'his shoe pinched him most painfully': marriage being the *shoo*.

494. *how soore I him twiste* 'how grievously I tormented him'.

495. *cam fro Jerusalem* 'returned from Jerusalem', after one of the three pilgrimages mentioned in *GP*, 465.

496. *the roode beem* A beam of timber spanning the chancel arch, and surmounted by a 'rood' or crucifix. To have buried her husband within the chancel itself would have been more expensive.

498. *of him Darius* 'of that man Darius'.

499. *Appelles* A Jewish craftsman to whom the tomb is ascribed in the *Alexandreid*, a Latin poem of the twelfth century. Skeat remarks that this tomb 'is due to fiction'.

500. *it nis but wast* 'it would have been simply extravagant'.

505. *the mooste shrewe* 'the cruellest person', or 'the cruellest of all the five'.

506. *al by rewe* 'one after another': cf. line 1254 below, 'a thousand time a-rewe'.

509. *so wel koude he me glose* 'he knew so well how to cajole and get round me'.

514. *of his love daungerous* 'offish and hard to please as a lover': cf. line 151 above and line 1090 below.

517. *waite what thing* 'whatever thing'.

518. *therafter wol we crie* 'we shall cry to be given it'.

520. *preesse on us faste* 'pursue us closely'.

521. *with daunger oute we al oure chaffare* 'as though reluctantly, we lay out all the goods we have to sell'.

522. *greet prees at market maketh deere ware* Proverbial: 'prices rise as the number of buyers increases'.

526. *and no richesse* 'not because he was wealthy', as her previous husbands had been.

528. *and hadde left scole* University studies are organized into various 'schools', or departments; those of medicine, divinity, mathematics, and so on. This 'clerk' or scholar had left Oxford,

probably lacking money to continue his studies; and seems to
have found employment as accountant or book-keeper to one
of the Wife's rich husbands, who would almost certainly have
been illiterate. Chaucer appears to have changed his conception of Jankin since describing him as 'oure apprentice' at
line 303 above.

    wente at hom to bord 'became a boarder in the house'. The
verb 'to board' seems not to have been current in Chaucer's
lifetime, and here *bord* refers to the table at which meals were
served. Cf. the remark about the rich carpenter of *The Miller's
Tale*, line 79, 'that gestes heeld to bord'.

530. *hir name was Alisoun* Like the Wife herself; see line 804
below.

532. *bet than oure parisshe preest* To whom the Wife would
periodically confess her sins. This suggests that her piety is
less sincere than her religious practices—described in *GP*,
451–2, 465–8—might imply.

534–5. *for hadde myn housbonde...cost his lyf* Whether he
committed a small offence or a capital crime.

543. *in a Lente* 'during Lent'; for the truly pious, a time of
fasting and solemn contemplation.

547. *to heere sondry talis* 'to pick up bits of gossip'. The
Wife's unseemly frivolity during Lent is matched by Chaucer's
pilgrims, who are hearing and relating 'sondry talis' during
April.

552–3. *to be seye of lusty folk* 'to be seen by people as lively and
pleasure-loving as herself'.

553–4. *what wiste I wher my grace was shapen for to be?* Chaucer
is playing ironically on two senses of *grace*. The Wife asks,
'How could I tell when and where I was fated to meet my
destined lover?' without recognizing that her question also
means, 'What did I care about my spiritual salvation at such a
time?'.

555. *I made my visitaciouns* 'I took part in'; cf. *RR*, 13725–8:

    Sovent voise à la mestre eglise,
    Et face visitacions
    A noces, à processions,
    A geus, à festes, à karoles.

556. *vigilies* 'vigils'; religious services held on the eve of a
saint's day. They are mentioned as a social attraction in
GP, 379.

processiouns Religious processions, probably at the annual exposure of a relic or effigy.

557. *to preching eek* The Pardoner's Prologue and Tale helps to explain the popularity of the medieval sermon—often preached in the open air—as a form of public entertainment.

thise pilgrimages The Wife is admitting what Chaucer has implied in the opening sentence of *GP*, that for most of its participants a pilgrimage was more an hilarious holiday excursion than a solemn act of devotion.

558. *pleyes of miracles* Miracle-plays, the popular drama of the age. Portraying events in a dramatic cycle from the Creation to the Last Judgement, these plays were a mixture of piety and broad farce, enlivened with figures derived from folk-lore as well as from religious sources.

mariages Weddings are still occasions for seeing and being seen, and for exchanging gossip.

559. *wered upon* 'wore'; the adverb indicating 'upon myself'.

561. *upon my peril* 'on peril of my soul'; a vigorous asseveration corresponding to 'I'll take my oath'.

562. *used weel* 'frequently worn', not stored away.

565. *daliance* 'banter', 'flirtatious talk'; a preliminary to embracing and love-making.

566. *of my purveiance* 'using my foresight'.

569. *for no bobance* 'not merely to boast'.

570–1. *withouten purveiance of mariage* 'without some matrimonial iron in the fire'.

572. *nat worth a leek* Such lively vernacular expressions characterize this last phase of Chaucer's development. Cf. line 1112 below, 'nat worth an hen'; *GP*, 182, 'nat worth an oystre'; and The Nun's Priest's Tale, line 24, 'nat worth a boterflye'.

573. *but oon hole for to sterte to* A proverbial figure, in ME and in French. Cf. *RR*, 13354–6:

> Moult a soris povre secors,
> En fait en grant peril sa druge,
> Qui n'a c'ung partuis à refuge.

574. *al ydo* 'everything finished'.

575. *enchanted me* 'given me a love-potion'. Chaucer is following La Vieille in *RR*, 13895: 'Si croi que m'avés enchantée'.

Notes

576. *my dame* Possibly 'my gossib, dame Alis', to whom the Wife has previously referred; or, more doubtfully, Venus. *The Pardoner's Tale* has 'thus taughte me my dame', in a different connexion. The expression may possibly be a proverbial form of reference to mother-wit.

578. *he wolde han slain me as I lay upright* The idea of this violent attack on the Wife in bed is intended to have another significance for Jankin.

580. *I hope that he shal do me good* The sudden change of tense and mood suggest that the Wife is mimicking herself making this coy remark to Jankin.

581. *blood bitokeneth gold* According to medieval dream-lore, blood and gold each signified the other. The Wife is making a broad hint of the money which comes with her.

582. *right naught* 'not at all'.

583. *my dames loore* 'my teacher's advice': see note to line 576 above. Mother-wit or womanly instinct seems to fit more appropriately than Dame Alice.

587. *on beere* 'on the bier', ready for burial.

588. *made sory cheere* 'behaved as though I were miserable'.

590. *coverchief* Or kerchief, a cloth covering for the head. *GP*, 455-7, describes the Wife's Sunday coverchief as weighing ten pounds. The scansion suggests that the word was already pronounced 'kerchief'.

591. *for that I was purveyed of a make* 'because I had provided myself with another husband'.

595. *oure clerk* Since the scholar Jankin does not live in the same house as the Wife, but boards with her gossip Alison (lines 528-9), this *oure* is probably not the possessive adjective. The phrase seems to confirm the suggestion that Jankin is employed by the Wife's husband in some secretarial capacity.

597. *after the beere* 'behind the bier', and the coffin.
 me thoughte 'it struck me'.

598. *so clene and faire* 'so shapely and attractive'.

599. *al myn herte I yaf unto his hoold* 'I lost my heart to him completely'. The Wife falls in love for the first time, and—ill-advisedly—surrenders herself and all her possessions to her lover.

600. *a twenty winter oold Winter* is here the plural form. OE neuter nouns with long stems were not inflected in the plural.

602. *a coltes tooth* 'Youthful in desires and inclinations': a proverbial expression, used by the Reeve in his *Prologue*, and

96

Notes

—in the form 'al coltissh'—in *The Merchant's Tale*.

603. *gat-tothed* 'having widely spaced teeth'; a feature mentioned in *GP*, 470.

604. *the prente of seinte Venus seel* As the Wife explains below, lines 609–13, the planet Venus was an important influence in her emotional make-up. By referring to a pagan goddess as 'St Venus', the Wife shows how the sacred and the profane are confused in her mind.

606. *wel bigon* 'well provided-for'. The Wife has inherited the estates of four husbands, at least three of whom were rich.

608. *the beste quoniam mighte be* 'the best you-know-what you could imagine'. The Wife is understandably pleased to repeat this basic compliment. Her Latin euphemism *quoniam*, meaning 'whereas', is probably chosen for its alliterative likeness to the blunter term she has previously used.

609–10. *al Venerien in feelinge* 'coming entirely under the influence of Venus in emotional character'.

610. *myn herte is Marcien* The Wife's heart, which is the source of vital spirits, comes under the influence of Mars. The combined effect of these two planetary influences is described in the two lines following.

613. *myn ascendent was Taur, and Mars therinne*. Briefly, the Wife was born when the zodiacal sign of Taurus, which is one of the houses of Venus, was rising and in power. But the benign influence of Venus was intercepted by the planet Mars, which was situated in Taurus at the time. Accordingly, the Wife's character was shaped by two entirely different and incompatible impulses: one pleasure-loving and promiscuous, the other boldly aggressive and domineering.

614. *that evere love was sinne!* This lament that sexual love should be considered sinful does not reveal a woman torn between the demands of physical appetite and her spiritual yearnings. The moment of uncharacteristic—and perhaps mock-serious—remorse quickly passes, and the Wife returns to her adventures, as buoyant as before.

616. *by vertu of my constellacioun* 'by force of the astrological influences which shaped my character'. Medieval science took these influences seriously, especially within the field of medicine: see *GP*, 416–20.

618. *my chambre of Venus* Yet another euphemism, probably taken from *RR*, 13540, 'la chambre Venus'.

Notes

a *good felawe* Cf. the use of the same expression in *GP*, 652 and 655. The literal meaning of the phrase is close to the modern 'good chap'; but evidently it could be used ironically to signify a dishonest or shady person. For *felawe* in the simple sense of 'friend, acquaintance', see line 758 below.

619. *Martes mark upon my face* The influence of Mars is seen in the Wife's 'gat-tothed' mouth, and in the ruddy complexion mentioned in *GP*, 460.

620. *in another privee place* Probably a red or purple birthmark on or near the pudendum. This may be the 'prente of seinte Venus seel' to which the Wife refers above, line 604.

622. *I ne loved nevere by no discrecioun* 'I never tried to be circumspect or discriminating in my love-affairs'. The sentence involves a triple-negative construction.

624. *al were he short, or long, or blak, or whit* 'whether he were short or tall, dark or fair'.

625. *so that he liked me* 'so long as he was attractive to me'.

626. *ne eek of what degree* 'nor to what social rank he belonged': possibly a sympathetic link with the Wife's Tale, especially lines 1109–76.

628. *so hende* The adjective *hende* has a great variety of meanings: skilful, clever; pleasant, courteous, gracious, kind, 'nice'; comely, agreeable to look at, and 'handy'. It is commonly applied to young men of the courtly or educated classes who are well turned-out, socially at ease, and practised in the arts of courtship and attendance on ladies. The Wife has noted Jankin's attractive appearance and obliging manners, and has hinted at his skill in flirtation. These qualities are all implicit in the term which she now applies to him.

629. *with greet solempnitee* 'with an impressive ceremony and great celebration'; in marked contrast to the inexpensive funeral given to her fourth husband a month earlier.

632. *repented me* 'it caused me to regret'.

633. *he nolde suffre nothing of my list* 'he would allow me none of the things I liked or wanted'. The line conveys the Wife's aggrieved tone as well as her actual complaint.

634. *the list* 'the ear'. The homophonous rhyme *list, list* shows the influence of French poetic convention upon Chaucer's writing. Earlier English poetry was based upon an alliterative tradition, derived from Anglo-Saxon, and made no use of rhyme. Chaucer follows the practice of medieval French poetry, which allowed half-rhymes and homophones such as

he uses here and in *GP*, 17–18, *seke, seeke*. See also lines 377–8 above, *housbonde, wives bonde*; lines 1067–8, *dampnacioun, nacioun*; and lines 1199–1200, *alenge, chalenge*. An appreciable number of weak rhymes occur in the present work, where only the final syllables of the two words accord: see for instance lines 223–4, *spitously, proprely*; lines 499–500, *subtilly, preciously*; and lines 883–4, *bacheler, river*.

635. *for that I rente out of his book a leef* The Wife speaks of her action as though it were inconsequential. But until the introduction of printing, books were both rare and expensive.

636. *myn ere wax al deef* The Wife's partial deafness is mentioned in *GP*, 448, without any explanation of its cause.

638. *a verray jangleresse* 'an indefatigable talker and gossip'. In a prologue of 850 lines the remark comes as no more than the truth.

640. *he had it sworn* 'he had sworn that I should not'.

642. *olde Romain geestes* 'tales from Roman history'. As noted above, line 460, Jankin's source is Valerius Maximus. His scholarship and his possession of a book make Jankin a much more formidable challenge to the Wife's authority than any of her previous husbands, who could only repeat proverbial sayings against women. The forces of Patristic and classical learning are now ranged against the Wife.

643. *he Simplicius Gallus* 'that man called Simplicius Gallus'.

645. *noght but for open-heveded he hir say* 'simply because he saw her with her hair uncovered'.

647. *another Romain* Whose story is told in the same chapter of Valerius.

648. *a someres game* A midsummer festival, celebrated with spectacles, processions, and a crude form of dramatic entertainment for which a summer-king and a summer-queen were elected. The festival evidently encouraged wild and dissolute behaviour, and attracted moral censure down to its suppression in the seventeenth century.

650. *upon his Bible seke* 'search in his Bible for'; cf. line 789, 'to reden on'.

651. *that ilke proverbe of Ecclesiaste* Ecclesiasticus xxv. 25: 'Give the water no passage; neither a wicked woman liberty to gad abroad'.

657. *to go seken halwes* 'to go on pilgrimage to holy places'; as in *GP*, 13–14, 'to seken...ferne halwes'. The remark provides further evidence of how doubtfully pilgrimages were regarded in Chaucer's lifetime.

659. *I sette noght an hawe* 'I didn't care a jot'.

661. *ne I wolde nat of him corrected be* 'nor would I allow
myself to be checked by him'.

665. *I nolde noght forbere him in no cas* 'I simply couldn't bring
myself to submit to him'.

666. *by Seint Thomas* Of Canterbury, whose shrine is the
object of the Wife's pilgrimage: a fact which makes the oath
particularly unfitting.

671. *Valerie and Theofraste* Two treatises against marriage:
the *Epistola Valerii ad Rufinum de non ducenda uxore*, by
Walter Map, and the *Liber de Nuptiis* by Theophrastus,
known from St Jerome's long quotation. Jankin's book is a
compilation of several anti-feminist works.

674. *Seint Jerome* One of the greatest scholars of the early
Christian Church, and author of the Vulgate, the Latin translation of the Bible. He recommended, and led, a life of
extreme asceticism. Although usually depicted as a cardinal
in medieval paintings, which show him with a lion at his feet,
there is no evidence that he held such office.

675. *a book again Jovinian* The *Epistola adversus Jovinianum*,
from which Chaucer appears to have borrowed the term
'octogamie' for line 33 above. Jovinian was an unorthodox
monk who died early in the fifth century, after being condemned
for denying that virginity was a higher state than marriage, and
that abstinence was better than thankful eating. His opinions
were attacked by St Augustine as well as by St Jerome.

676. *Tertulan* Probably Tertullian, an early Roman convert to
Christiantity, whose treatises on chastity, monogamy and
modesty would find a fitting place in Jankin's collection.

677. *Crisippus* A writer mentioned by St Jerome, who remarks
that it was absurd of Crisippus to advise the wise man to
marry in order to placate the deity of marriage and increase.
Nothing more is known of him.

  Trotula Thought to be a distinguished gynaecologist, or
possibly a midwife, practising at Salerno about the middle of
the eleventh century. She was credited with having written a
treatise on the diseases of women, another on cosmetics, *De
ornatu mulierum*, and a third on feminine passions.

  Helowis Heloïse, secret wife of the great teacher and priest
Abélard, and later prioress of the convent of Argenteuil,
about ten miles from the centre of Paris. She is described as
abéesse in *RR*.

Notes

679. *the Parables of Salomon* The Book of Proverbs.

680. *Ovides Art* The *Ars Amatoria*, written early in the first century. Ovid recommends ways of succeeding in love, mocking the style of other books of instruction. The work is enlivened by anecdotes.

685. *this book of wikked wives* Jankin's compilation hardly deserves this description, even if *wives* means mature women like the Wife herself rather than married ones. The theme of the book is rather the moral weakness and dangerous attraction of woman, which make her a snare for man.

686. *lives* 'biographies'.

688. *trusteth wel* 'believe me'.
    an impossible 'an impossibility'.

689. *that any clerk wol speke good of wives* The Wife's remark is justified by the antagonism of early Christian and medieval authorities towards woman, the cause of man's original sin and Fall. Thus Tertullian could write to his 'beloved sisters', 'You are the gateway of the devil, you are the unsealer of the forbidden tree, you are the first rebel against the divine law'.

691. *never the mo* 'never at all'.

692. *who peyntede the leon?* 'Alluding to the fable in Aesop, where a sculptor represented a man conquering a lion. The lion's criticism was to the effect that he had heard of cases in which the lion conquered the man' (Skeat). The Wife interprets her remark in lines 693–6 following.

694. *withinne hire oratories* Suggesting the seclusion which protects the scholar from contact with the realities of everyday life.

696. *al the mark of Adam* 'all beings made like Adam'; 'men'.

697. *the children of Mercurie and of Venus* Those born under the influence of these two planets; scholars and attractive women respectively.

698. *in hir wirking ful contrarius* 'completely different in behaviour and outlook'.

699. *science* Knowledge acquired by study, without limitation to subjects now called scientific.

700. *riot and dispence* 'unrestrained enjoyment and extravagance'.

701. *for hire diverse disposicioun* 'by reason of their contrary natures'.

702. *ech falleth in otheres exaltacioun* The influence of either planet is weakest when the other enjoys its position of

Notes

greatest power, or exaltation.

703–4. *Mercurie is desolat in Pisces, wher Venus is exaltat* Within the zodiacal sign of Pisces, Mercury has its dejection, and Venus her exaltation.

706. *therfore no womman of no clerk is preysed* The antipathy between Venus and Mercury extends to the particular natures —the pleasure-loving and the studious—produced by the influence of these planets. This explains why no scholar can bring himself to speak well of woman.

708. *Venus werkes* making love.

worth his olde sho Compare the similar expression at line 572 above and note.

709. *and writ in his dotage* 'and writes in his senile folly'.

710. *kepe hir mariage* 'observe their marriage-vows', 'remain faithful'.

711. *but now to purpose* This is the Wife's third attempt to reach the climax of her story, already briefly related in lines 634–5 and re-introduced in lines 666–8. Another eighty lines of her Prologue must pass before she at last rewards her audience's patience with a detailed account of the event. The Nun's Priest is made to employ a similar narrative technique of repeatedly digressing from his Tale.

tolde thee The intimate pronoun gives the narrative a more confidential tone, as though the Wife were gathering her audience more closely about her.

713. *oure sire* 'the head of the household', Jankin.

715. *of Eva first, that for hir wikkednesse* 'first about Eve, through whose sin of plucking the forbidden fruit'.

716. *broght to wrecchednesse* Compare Milton,

> Whose mortal taste
> Brought death into the world, and all our woe.
>
> (*Paradise Lost*, I. 2, 3)

718. *herte blood* 'heart's blood', hence 'life'.

719. *expres of womman* 'explicitly stated about women'.

720. *was the los of al mankinde* 'caused a disaster which affected all mankind'.

721. *how Sampson loste his heres* See Judges xvi. 17–19, and *The Monk's Tale*, stanzas 9–11. The story of Samson and Delilah also figures in the *Epistola Valerii*.

725. *Hercules and of his Dianire* Deianira, wife of Hercules, gave him the shirt of Nessus as a means of renewing his love for her, unaware that the shirt was poisoned. To escape his agony, Hercules allowed his body to be consumed by fire.

727. *no thing forgat he* 'he omitted no detail of'.

728. *Socrates* Philosopher of ancient Greece, 469–399 B.C. This apocryphal story of his married life comes from St Jerome's *Epistola adversus Jovinianum*. It was repeated by Erasmus in his *Apophthegms*.

732. *er that thonder stinte, comth a reyn* 'rain has to fall before the thunder will stop'.

734. *for shrewednesse, him thoughte the tale swete* 'as an example of wickedness, this seemed to him a fine story'.

736. *hire horrible lust and hir liking* Pasiphäe, wife of Minos of Crete, became enamoured of a bull and allowed him to father upon her a monstrous offspring, the Minotaur. Pasiphäe, Clytemnestra and Eriphyle are mentioned together in a single sentence of the *Epistola adversus Jovinianum*, shortly after the story of Socrates.

737. *Clitermystra* Clytemnestra, wife of Agammemnon, took a lover during her husband's long absence as commander of the Greek forces at Troy. At his return she murdered Agammemnon in his bath with an axe.

738. *that falsly made hire housbonde for to die* 'who treacherously killed her husband'.

739. *with ful good devocioun* 'most attentively'.

740. *for what occasioun* 'by what circumstances'.

741. *Amphiorax* Amphiaraus. His wife Eriphyle was bribed with a necklace to secure his support in the expedition of the Seven against Thebes, during which he was killed.

746. *sory grace* 'misfortune'. After being repulsed from the city walls, he was swallowed up in a cleft made by a thunderbolt.

747. *Livia* Livilla, who poisoned her husband Drusus at the instigation of her lover Sejanus, A.D. 23.

Lucie Lucilia, wife of Lucretius, poet and philosopher of the first century B.C. Both women are mentioned in the *Epistola Valerii*.

749. *that oon..., that oother* 'one of them, the other'.

750. *on an even late* 'late at night'.

751. *she was his fo* 'she hated him'. Lucretius ignored her in the absorption of his work.

753. *for he sholde* 'in order to cause him'.

754. *swich a manere* 'such a (powerful) form of'.

755. *it were by the morwe* 'by the time morning arrived'.

757. *oon Latumius* 'a man called Latumius'. The story of the hanging-tree had a wide circulation, appearing in works by Cicero and Erasmus as well as in the *Epistola Valerii* and the medieval *Gesta Romanorum*. In a different form it was later used by Shakespeare in *Timon of Athens*.

761. *for herte despitus* 'out of bitterness of heart'.

765. *of latter date* 'later on'.

768. *in the floor upright* 'stretched out on the floor, face upwards'. Cf. line 796 below.

769. *drive nailes in hir brain* As Sisera did to Jael; see Judges iv. 21.

772. *than herte may bithinke* 'than mind can imagine'. The Wife is using *herte* in a general sense which includes the faculties of feeling and expression: cf. line 761 above, note.

775–6. '*Bet is thyn habitacioun be*' 'it is better to live with'. The remark follows Ecclesiasticus xxv. 16 very closely.

777. *usinge for to chide* 'habitually nagging'.

778. *hye in the roof* 'up in the attic': cf. *The Miller's Tale*, line 457, 'hange hem in the roof ful hye'. Jankin is quoting Proverbs xxi. 9.

781. *they haten that hir housbondes loven ay* 'they always hate whatever gives their husbands pleasure'.

783. *whan she cast of hir smok* 'when she throws off her last piece of clothing': see *The Clerk's Tale*, lines 876–88.

784–5. '*A fair womman...sowes nose*' Again quoting from Proverbs, here xi. 22. The Parson repeats the allusion in his Tale: 'Likneth a fair womman that is a fool of hire body lyk to a ring of gold that were in the groin of a soughe'.

786. *who wolde suppose* 'who could imagine'.

789. *to reden on* 'to read'.

790. *thre leves* In her two previous references to the occasion, lines 635 and 667, the Wife has admitted to plucking only one page out of Jankin's book. Now that she has reached the climax of her Tale she is prepared to reveal the full extent of her crime.

793. *in oure fyr he fil bakward adoun* 'he fell over backwards into the fire'. The representative of authority is overthrown in a scene of knockabout farce. For *oure fyr* see note on line 311.

797. *he saugh how stille that I lay* The Wife's 'swogh' does not prevent her from observing Jankin's behaviour.

798. *wolde han fled his way* 'would have taken to his heels'. The Wife recovers consciousness just in time to prevent this, which suggests that she had been shamming.

801. *for my land thus hastow mordred me?* By this tactical master-stroke the Wife throws Jankin completely off-balance and seizes the moral advantage from him; entirely ignoring the fact that she struck the first blow. This show of intellectual 'maistrie' follows the technique she describes in lines 389–92 above.

803. *kneled faire adoun* Apparently sardonic: 'kneeled down nicely', or perhaps 'submissively'.

804. *suster* 'sister': in the sense of a fellow-member of a church or society.

806. *it is thyself to wite* 'you have yourself to blame': meaning that he would not strike her unprovoked.

807. *and that I thee biseke* The phrase *and that* gives emphasis to the request: 'I beg you most sincerely'. Cf. line 850 below: 'Pees! and that anon!' meaning, 'be quiet at once, this minute'.

809. *thus muchel am I wreke* 'I have this much revenge'.

812. *we fille acorded by us selven two* 'we came to an agreement between the two of us'.

814. *to han the governance of hous and lond* thus retrieving the mistake she had made on marrying Jankin: see lines 630–1.

815. *of his tonge, and of his hond also* she was to have the right of veto over what he said and did; *his hond* perhaps referring to chastisement.

816. *anon right tho* 'on the spot, there and then'. Without the destruction of 'this cursed book' the Wife cannot breathe freely, for it symbolizes the force of authority which has baffled her hitherto. Now she can face Jankin on even footing.

818. *by maistrie* 'by proving her superiority'; physically, through combat; intellectually, by showing greater cunning and quickness of wit, and through strength of will.

    soverainetee 'supremacy', 'power of human authority and overlordship'.

820. *do as thee lust the terme of al thy lyf* 'do just as you please, for as long as you live'.

821. *keep thyn honour, and keep eke myn estaat* 'guard your moral reputation and respect my standing in society'.

Jankin's conditions conform closely with the terms accepted by the Knight at the end of the Wife's Tale; see lines 1232-3 below.

825. *and also trewe* 'and just as faithful'.

826. *that sit* 'who sits'.

827. *so blesse* 'therefore to bless'.

829. *the Frere lough* The Friar is described in *The General Prologue* as outwardly genial and a good mixer. His laughing appreciation of the Wife's 'long preamble' is typical of his relaxed and indulgent manner towards the affluent. So too is his ingratiating form of address, which reflects his wide acquaintance with 'worthy wommen of the toun' (*GP*, 217). But the Wife is not taken in by his charming behaviour, and snubs him.

830. *now dame* Repeating the polite form of address used by the Pardoner at line 164 above, and properly applicable to women of higher social rank.

   so have I 'as I wish to have'.

833. *Goddes armes two!* The violent oath suggests the character of the man whom *The General Prologue* describes as noisy, terrifyingly ugly, and completely corrupt.

834. *wol entremette him everemo* 'will be forever interfering'. This exchange shows how little love was lost between friars and other clerics.

836. *wol falle in every dissh* 'likes to drop into every dish'. This part of the proverbial saying certainly fits the Friar, who makes a point of becoming well acquainted with gourmets: see *GP*, 215-16.

837. *preambulacioun* Presumably 'making a preamble'; a term coined for the occasion. The Summoner habitually talks nonsense when he tries to air his knowledge of technical jargon: see *GP*, 641-2:

> A few termes hadde he, two or thre,
> That he had lerned out of som decree.

838. *amble, or trotte* Mistaking the sense of 'preamble' for the more familiar term which it contains.

   or pees 'or be quiet'.

839. *thou lettest oure disport* 'you interrupt our amusement'.

840. *ye, woltow so?* 'so that's how you want it?'. The Friar now reveals the spiteful nature usually hidden by his charm and effusiveness.

Notes

843. *alle the folk shal laughen in this place* 'all the pilgrims about us here will burst out laughing'. At the conclusion of the Wife's Tale the Friar tells a story of a wicked summoner who is carried off by the devil after trying to cheat an old woman.

846. *but if I* 'if I don't'. This squabble enlivens the closing moments of the Wife's Prologue. It also provides the motivation of the two tales to follow, and gives the group a connecting link.

846–7. *tales two or thre of freres* After *The Friar's Tale*, the Summoner tells the story of a grasping friar whose greed leads him to seize an unsavoury bequest. Both he and the Friar promise to tell more than one tale, following the Host's original proposal (*GP*, 793–6) that each pilgrim shall relate four tales in all. This proposal is later retracted.

847. *Sidingborne* Sittingbourne; a town 40 miles from London and 15 from Canterbury, where the pilgrims might have planned to spend one of their nights on the road.

849. *thy pacience is gon* A warning that the Friar will not be able to bear so much ridicule.

850. *oure Hooste cride 'Pees!'* As elected leader of the company, the Host has the task of checking unruly pilgrims and of generally preserving good relations among its members.

852. *that dronken ben* 'who are drunk'.

853. *do, dame* 'proceed, madam'. The Host is directing her to begin, not courteously imploring.

854. *right as yow lest* 'just as you please'.

856. *Yis* An emphatic affirmative: 'by all means'.

859. *al was this land fulfild, of faierie* 'there were fairies in every corner of the realm': supernatural beings having the size and general appearance of ordinary men and women.

860. *elf-queene* 'the queen of fairies'.

862. *as I rede* 'as I understand'.

866. *limitours* 'limiters'; friars licensed to beg within a specified district, like the Friar himself: see *GP*, 209. The Wife is beginning a satirical digression which will put the Friar in his place. Her reference to 'grete charitee and prayeres' in the previous line is entirely sardonic.

867. *that serchen* 'who visit'; but the suggestion of searching is apposite, since the Friar is making an avaricious quest for money.

869. *blessinge* Again ironic. The friars were predominantly concerned with wringing money out of the faithful, by whatever means. The catalogue of places which they visit—

kitchens, bedrooms, stables, farms—suggests their impudent intrusiveness.

872. *this maketh that ther ben no faieries* 'this widespread "blessing" is responsible for there being no more fairies'. The greater supernatural power of Christianity has evidently exorcised them. Cf. *The Miller's Tale*, 371–8, where the carpenter tries to release Nicholas from his supposed enchantment by invoking the powers of religion.

873. *ther as wont to walken was an elf* 'in the place previously frequented by fairies'.

876. *hooly thinges* 'devotions'. This sense of 'thing', something said or uttered, appears again in *thinges smale*, 'short tales', at line 952 below.

877. *in his limitacioun* 'in his appointed district'.

878. *wommen may go now saufly up and doun* A common motif of folk-lore concerns the seizing of a young woman by a supernatural being who forces her to live with him in the greenwood, and to bear his children. The Wife remarks that this particular danger no longer exists.

880. *incubus* Strictly, a male spirit popularly supposed to have sexual intercourse with sleeping women. Here the Wife must be alluding to the fairy lover of folk-lore, and also suggesting an additional activity of the friars.

881. *he ne wol doon hem but dishonour* The fairy lover fathered actual children upon his human partner. The Friar merely brings dishonour upon the women he seduces. The Wife is striking home: see *GP*, 213, and note.

883. *in his hous* 'among his entourage'.
    bacheler a knight without land.

884. *fro river* 'from hawking for water-fowl'.

885. *as he was born* 'as he rode'.

887. *maugree hir heed* 'despite all she could do'. The Knight's complete lack of courteous respect for women starts the adventure which ends in his yielding himself completely to his wife's will.

891. *dampned...for to be deed* 'condemned to death'.

893. *swich was the statut tho* 'such was the law at the time'. Chaucer feels obliged to explain an unlikely circumstance which—as in *Measure for Measure*—forms a necessary condition of the story.

895. *preyeden the king of grace* 'begged the king to show clemency'.

896. *in the place* 'on the spot, without going away'.

897. *al at hir wille* 'at her complete discretion'.

902. *in swich array* 'in such a plight'.

903. *suretee* 'certainty'. At line 911 below the same term means 'guarantee of return'.

904. *if thou kanst tellen me* The posing of the 'life-question' which follows is a common theme of medieval romance, with analogues in older literature. The Knight's unmotivated crime is a necessary element of the story, bringing him under sentence of death and so allowing the 'life-question' to be put to him. The story proper then begins.

906. *keep thy nekke-boon from iren!* 'keep the axe from your neck!'.

909–10. *to seche and leere an answere suffisant* 'to seek out and discover a satisfactory answer'.

912. *thy body for to yelden* 'to give yourself up at the end of the year'.

914. *he may nat do al as him liketh* 'he has little choice in the matter'.

915. *he chees him* 'he chooses'.

922. *he ne koude arriven in no coost* 'he could not discover any country'.

924. *accordinge in-feere* 'agreeing together'.

926. *honour* 'dignified position'.

927. *lust abedde* 'sexual pleasure'.

929. *oure hertes* The Wife allows her own interest in the subject to appear.

931. *he gooth ful ny the sothe* 'he comes very close to the truth'.

934. *been we ylimed, bothe moore and lesse* 'we are caught, whatever our rank'. The Wife's Tale has now developed into an appendix to her discussion of feminine character in her Prologue. Lines 929–50 form a personal comment rather than part of the story.

936. *right as us lest* 'just as it pleases us'.

937. *repreve us of oure vice* 'rebuke us for our misbehaviour'. The Wife has returned to a theme of her Prologue: cf. lines 662–3 above.

938. *no thing nice* 'not at all foolish'.

939. *noon of us alle* 'not one of us'.

940. *clawe us on the galle* 'rub us on a sore spot'.

941. *that we nel kike, for he seith us sooth* 'that we won't lash out in irritation at being told the plain truth': literally, 'because he tells us the truth'.

942. *that so dooth* 'whoever does so'.

946. *for to been holden stable* 'to be considered constant'.

949. *nat worth a rake-stele* Another characteristically vigorous expression. The Wife's scorn is explained by lines 538–42 above.

950. *no thing hele* 'keep nothing secret'.

951. *witnesse on Mida* 'look at Midas, for example'.

952. *Ovide* Ovid, previously mentioned as the author of the *Ars Amatoria*, line 680 above. The 'othere thinges smale' mentioned by the Wife refers to the great collection of classical myths involving transformation, which forms the poet's *Metamorphoses*.

954. *two asses eres* The more famous story of Midas concerns the gift of the golden touch, bestowed upon him by Bacchus in return for the king's hospitality. The asses' ears were set upon him when Midas judged Pan a better musician than Apollo.

957. *save his wyf* According to Ovid, the secret was known only to Midas' barber, who whispered it into a hole dug in the ground. Chaucer alters the story to suit the Wife's purposes.
ther wiste of it namo 'no other person knew of it'.

961. *she swoor him nay* 'she swore she would not'.

961–2. *al this world to winne, she nolde* 'not for the world would she'.

965. *hir thoughte that she dide* 'it seemed to her that she would die'.

967. *it swal so soore* 'the secret oppressed her so painfully'.

968. *nedely som word hire moste asterte* 'some hint of the truth simply must break through her guard'.

972. *as a bitore bombleth in the mire* 'as a bittern booms in the fen'; supposedly by extending its long beak over the surface of the water. In fact, when it makes this call the bittern's head and bill are pointed directly upwards.

974. *biwreye me nat* The barber's secret was revealed when reeds grew out of the hole into which he had whispered, and repeated his story in their rustling. The Wife's version of the story does not require this *dénouement*.

977. *al hool* 'completely sound, cured'.

978. *I myghte no lenger kepe it* 'I couldn't have kept the secret any longer'. Compare the Wife's indiscretions, lines 534–8.
out of doute 'that's certain'.

979–80. *thogh we a time abide, yet out it moot* 'though we can keep a secret for a short while, it must eventually come out'.

982. *redeth* 'read'; the polite imperative.

983. *specially* 'particularly concerned with'.

984. *come therby* 'gain possession or knowledge of it'.

986. *the goost* 'his spirit'.

989. *it happed him to ride* 'he chanced to ride'.

991. *upon a daunce go* 'dancing', probably in a ring; a familiar element of Celtic folk-tales. The dancers are of course fairies.

993. *he drow ful yerne* 'he advanced eagerly'.

996. *this daunce* 'the circle of dancers'.

1000. *again the knight* [she] *gan rise* 'she rose and faced him'. The auxiliary *gan* has a function like that of 'did' in modern English.

1001. *heer forth ne lith no wey* 'go no further'; literally, 'this road leads nowhere'.

1004. *thise olde folk kan muchel thing* 'old people understand many things'. For another example of *thise* in a generalizing sense see line 560 above.

1006. *I nam but deed* 'if not, I'm a dead man'.

1008. *I wolde wel quite youre hire* 'I would repay your service generously'.

1009. *plight me thy trouthe* 'pledge me your solemn word'.
    heere in myn hand The verbal promise is to be confirmed by 'handfasting'.

1015. *I wol stonde therby* 'I assure you'.

1017. *lat se* Literally, 'let one see' = 'show me'.
    proudeste 'grandest', 'highest in rank'.

1018. *that wereth on* 'who wears'; repeating the construction used at line 559 above, and speaking periphrastically of women.

1021. *a pistel* 'a message'; the answer to the life-question.

1024. *he had holde his day* 'he had kept his undertaking to return on that day'.

1025. *as he sayde* 'as he ventured'. The verb is from *sayen*, 'to endeavour or essay', not from *seyen*, 'to say or speak'.

1027. *for that they been wise* 'because widows are wise' (and therefore qualified to judge the Knight's answer). The Wife would think so.

1028. *as a justice* 'as president of the court'. Courts of love presided over by ladies were actually held in the Middle Ages, though not to determine matters of life and death.

1033–4. The homophonous rhyme *best best* was allowed because two different senses were involved. See the general note on line 634 above.

Notes

1037. *generally* 'everywhere'.

1040. *for to been in maistrie him above* 'to have the upper hand in her dealings with him'.

1041. *thogh ye me kille* 'even though you kill me for saying so'.

1046. *the olde wyf* 'the old woman'; unmarried, as her request proves.

1048. *mercy* The cry of a petitioner for a sympathetic hearing.

1055. *me take unto thy wyf* 'marry me'.

1057. *sey nay* 'contradict me'.

1060. *as chees a newe requeste* 'make some other request'. In ME *as* is sometimes used to emphasize an imperative verb. Compare *The Nun's Priest's Tale*, line 177, 'as taak som laxatif'.

1061. *lat my body go* 'release me'.

1065. *that under erthe is grave* 'buried underground'.

1066. *but if thy wyf I were* 'unless I were your wife'. The Lady is completing the asseveration begun two lines earlier, where *I nolde* = 'I refuse to'.
   and eek thy love 'not only your legal spouse but your darling'.

1067. *my dampnacioun* Ironic: since the Lady has rescued the Knight when he was 'dampned...for to be deed'.

1068. *that any of my nacioun* 'that a man of my high birth'.

1069. *so foule disparaged* 'so shamefully dishonoured'.

1071. *he nedes moste* 'he was compelled to'.

1074. *for my necligence I do no cure* 'out of carelessness I overlook'.

1079. *ther nas but hevinesse* 'there was nothing but depression'.

1081. *hidde him as an owle* 'avoided company': the owl shuns daylight.

1082. *so wo was him* Literally, 'such misery was to him'; in modern English, 'so miserable he was'. As in the expression, 'woe is me', the personal pronoun takes the dative.

1083. *in his thoght* 'in his mind'.

1084. *abedde ybroght* 'brought to bed'. After the marriage-feast the celebrations ended in the bridal chamber, where the guests saw the bridal pair put to bed. See *The Merchant's Tale*,

> The bride was broght abedde as stille as stoon;
> And whan the bed was with the preest yblessed,
> Out of the chambre hath every wight him dressed
> [= 'betaken himself'].

Notes

1085. *he walweth and he turneth to and fro* Recalling the miserable plight of the Wife's old husbands, who 'many a night... songen "Weilaway!"'.

1090. *is every knight of his so dangerous?* When the Knight should have been sexually reserved he had dishonoured himself. Marriage to a physically repulsive wife is proper retribution for his offence against the standards of knightly conduct.

1092. *which that saved hath* 'who saved'.

1093. *yet ne dide I yow nevere unright* 'I have never done you wrong'.

1095. *had lost his wit* 'who was out of his mind'.

1099. *it wol nat been amended nevere mo* 'it can never be altered'.

1100. *so loothly* 'so hideously repulsive'. Chaucer happens to use the term which is now used to identify the literary type of his character, the Loathly Lady. Such characters appear in other tales of the period.

1101. *of so lough a kinde* 'from such base stock'.

1103. *so wolde God* 'would to God'.

1107. *er it were dayes thre* 'before three days had passed', 'in a short while'.

1108. *so wel ye mighte bere yow unto me* 'with such effect that you would behave very respectfully towards me'.

1109. *for ye speken of* 'since you mention'. The Knight has not in fact referred directly to the subject; but the long digression which follows, amounting to a quarter of the Tale, shows Chaucer's interest in a topic which—as the Lady's argument admits—had been seriously treated by a number of medieval poets. Chaucer's argument is summed up in four lines of his *Romaunt of the Rose*, 2189–92:

> To clepe no wight in noo ages
> Oonly gentil for his linages;
> But whoso is vertuous,
> And in his port nought outrageous.

gentillesse 'nobility, distinction'. Modern English possesses no exact equivalent for this important medieval term, which is considered at greater length in the appropriate section of *An Introduction to Chaucer*. A sense of its meaning here emerges from the discussion itself.

1111. *that therfore sholden ye be gentil men* 'that you should be considered gentlemen on account of your rich ancestors'.

113

1113. *looke who* 'whoever'.

1114. *privee and apert* 'both in private and in public'.

1115. *to do the gentil dedes that he kan* 'to behave as nobly and courteously as he is able'.

1117. *Crist wole we claime of him oure gentillesse* 'Christ wishes us to derive our virtuous qualities from him': an idea borrowed from Dante, repeated in the quotation at line 1130 below.

1120. *to been of heigh parage* 'to have noble ancestry'.

1121. *for no thing* 'by no means whatever'.

1122. *hir vertuous living* 'their virtuous habit of life'.

1123. *gentil men* Here the term implies courteous, decent and considerate behaviour. Originally, *gentil* referred to noble rank, but came to have a wider application. The Lady's argument shows Chaucer helping to extend the meaning of the term.

1124. *in swich degree* 'in the same fashion' in manner of life, not merely in the assumption of noble rank.

1125. *the wise poete of Florence* Dante Alighieri, 1265–1321, the greatest of medieval poets. Chaucer borrowed much from him. Here, against all likelihood, both the Lady and the Wife of Bath are being credited with a knowledge of *The Divine Comedy* and of the *Convivio*, an unfinished work on philosophy, so that Chaucer may develop some of Dante's ideas. The fairy-tale and the Wife's pragmatic outlook both recede into the background.

1125–6. *wel kan* [he] *speken in this sentence* Dante puts it admirably in this observation.

1127. *in swich maner rym is Dantes tale* 'Dante's comment is set in rhymed verses, like this'. The lines occur in the *Purgatorio*, VII, 121–3:

> Rade volte risurge per li rami
> l'umana probitate: e questo vuole
> quei che la dà, perchè da lui si chiami.

1128. *by his branches smale* Dante speaks of *probitate*, 'moral integrity', rising *through* the branches which represent the heirs of noble stock. Chaucer's rendering does not make this clear.

1130. *wole that* 'desires that'; as in line 1117 above.

1132. *that man may hurte and maime* 'that may be damaged or injured'. *Man* is used impersonally, as in modern German.

Notes

1134. *planted natureelly* 'implanted as an innate quality'.

1135. *unto a certeyn linage doun the line* 'within a particular family through descent'.

1137. *to doon of gentillesse the faire office* 'to perform all the praiseworthy actions that appertain to a gentleman'.

1138. *they mighte do no vileynie* 'they would be incapable of any discourteous or shameful act'.

1139. *ber it in* 'carry it into'.

1140. *bitwix this* 'between this place'.

   mount of Kaukasous 'the Caucasian mountains': the first of several ideas taken from the *Consolations of Philosophy* of Boethius, which Chaucer translated as *Boece*. A reference to 'the mountaigne that highte Caucasus', describing it as one of the furthest points to which the fame of Rome had spread, appears at II. pr. 7. 62 of Chaucer's translation.

1142. *lie and brenne* 'blaze vigorously'.

1143. *as twenty thousand men mighte it biholde* 'as though thousands of people were watching it'.

1144. *his office natureel ay wol it holde* 'it will continue to behave in accordance with its proper nature'. Chaucer had come across the comparison in Boethius: 'Certes yif that honour of peple were a natureel gifte to dignites, it ne mighte nevere cesen nowhere amonges no maner folk to don his office; right as fyer in every contre ne stinteth nat to eschaufen [does not cease to burn] and to ben hoot' (*Boece*, III. pr. 4. 64–9).

1145. *up peril of my lyf* 'I'm ready to swear'.

1146–7. *genterie is nat annexed to possessioun* 'nobility is not dependent upon wealth'.

1148–9. *no doon hir operacioun alwey* 'do not constantly observe the laws which should govern their behaviour'.

1149. *in his kinde* 'according to its nature'. Medieval scientists believed that natural phenomena were determined not by physical laws but by impulses within objects themselves; light things desiring to ascend, and heavy ones to fall.

1150. *wel often* 'frequently'.

1152. *that wol han pris of his gentrie* 'who wishes to be respected for his high birth'.

1155. *nel himselven* 'will not himself'. In OE both parts of the pronoun were inflected. This practice is often carried over into ME: compare *us selven* at line 812 above.

1157. *he nis nat gentil, be he duc or erl* The idea is repeated very closely in the *Ballade of Gentillesse*, lines 13–14.

Notes

1158. *vileyns sinful dedes make a cherl* 'a man is to be considered a churl if he behaves like a villein'. Compare Chaucer's *Romaunt of the Rose*, 2181–2:

> For vilanie makith vilayn,
> And by his dedis a cherl is seyn.

Churls and villeins formed the lowest rank of medieval society, labouring in the humblest occupations. From the coarseness of their manners, both terms came to be used as opprobrious epithets. *Cherl* is applied in this sense at line 460 above. The acts of a villein might be considered villainous in two senses of the word. When Chaucer appeals to his audience in *The General Prologue*,

> N'arette it nat my vileinye,
> Thogh that I pleynly speke in this mateere,   (728–9)

he is asking not to be judged a villain even though, in repeating a churl's tale, he must speak like a villein.

1159. *thy gentillesse* The Lady now deals specifically with the claim which, at line 1109 above, she asserts the Knight to have made. The present text adopts the suggestion made by J. S. Kenyon, that the initial words of lines 1159 and 1162 should be exchanged. The MSS read *For gentillesse nis* and *Thy gentillesse cometh*.

1160. *for hire heigh bountee* 'acquired by their great virtue'.

1161. *a strange thing to thy persone* 'not an integral part of yourself'. Compare *Boece*, III. pr. 6. 34 ff.: 'Yif the name of gentilesse be referred to renoun and cleernesse of linage, thanne is gentil name but a foreyn thing...Foreyn gentilesse ne maketh the nat gentil'.

1163. *thanne comth oure verray gentillesse of grace* 'true nobility is a grace derived from God'.

1164. *biquethe us with oure place* 'bequeathed to us with our social rank'.

1165. *as seith Valerius* The author quoted by Jankin: see line 671, and notes to lines 460, 643 and 647 above. The Wife's acquaintance with Valerius is explained by Jankin's scholarship, but nothing accounts for this quoting of a Roman author by a folk-lore figure. Her injunction to the Knight to study Boethius and Seneca, at line 1168 below, is still more incongruous. Chaucer has lost sight of the speaker's fairy character in the interest of his philosophical discussion.

1166. *Tullius Hostillius* From the humblest of origins, and after being a herdsman in early life, he rose to become ruler of the Roman state, and to enjoy in his old age the highest honours and dignities.

1168. *reedeth...redeth* 'study', 'grasp the meaning of'. Both are forms of the verb *reden* which—as though reflecting the general illiteracy of the times—does not often mean 'to read': see, for instance, line 862 above, where it cannot have this meaning.

  Senek Seneca, Roman philosopher and dramatist who died in A.D. 65.

  Boece Boethius, whose philosophical work was written in prison before his execution in A.D. 525.

1169. *it no drede is* 'it is beyond dispute'.

1172. *al were it that* 'although'.

1175. *thanne am I gentil, whan that I biginne* 'I am to be considered gentle when I begin'.

1177. *and ther as ye* 'and where you'. The accusation is baseless.

1182. *a vicious living* 'an immoral way of life'.

1183. *glad poverte* 'being content with limited means'. Chaucer is paraphrasing Seneca in *Epist.* ii. 4: 'Honesta, inquit, res est laeta paupertas' ('happy poverty is an honorable thing').

1184. *this wole...clerkes seyn* 'scholars support this view'.

1185. *that halt him paid* 'who considers himself contented'; more simply, 'who feels content'.

1186. *I holde him riche* Continuing the paraphrase of Seneca: 'Cui enim cum paupertate bene convenit, dives est' ('whoever reconciles himself with his poverty is rich').

1187. *he that coveiteth is a povre wight* 'Non qui parum habet, sed qui plus cupit, pauper est' ('not the man who has little, but he who covets to have more, is the poor man'). The disparity of outlook between the Wife of Bath and her tale is particularly marked here. One of the Wife's confessed principles of life is to seize and hold all the wealth she can lay hands on.

1188. *that is nat in his might* 'the thing which he cannot possess' —content.

1189. *ne coveiteth have* 'nor covets to have'.

1190. *but a knave* 'only a menial'.

1191. *it singeth proprely* 'it sings of its own nature'.

1192. *Juvenal* Roman satirist of the first century A.D. The reference is to Satire, x, 21: 'Cantabit vacuus coram latrone viator. The comment recurs in Dante's *Convivio*, and in Chaucer's *Boece*.

1193. *goth by the weye* 'passes along the road'.

1195. *hateful good* 'an unattractive blessing'; painful, but spiritually beneficial. The same idea occurs in *Piers Plowman*, B-text, xiv. 275: 'Paupertas,' quod Pacience, 'est odibile bonum'.

1197. *a greet amendere eek of sapience* 'also a great improver of wisdom'.

1200. *possessioun that no wight wol chalenge* 'a thing which no one asks to possess'.

1202. *maketh his God and eek himself to knowe* 'teaches him to know himself and his God'.

1203. *as thinketh me* 'it seems to me'.

1205. *sin that I noght yow greve* 'since I give you no cause for complaint'. The Knight has objected to her ugliness, old age and base stock, and not against any moral failing.

1207. *of elde* 'of being old'.

1208-9. *thogh noon auctoritee were in no book* 'even if there were no textual authority for this opinion'. The remark runs very close to the form of the Wife's opening assertion, 'though noon auctoritee were in this world'.

1209. *ye gentils of honour* 'persons of noble reputation'. Possibly *ye* should be read as *yet*.

1210. *sholde an oold wight doon favour* 'should behave respectfully towards the aged'. Cf. *The Pardoner's Tale*, 453-4:

It is no curteisye
To speken to an old man vileynye.

1211. *for youre gentillesse* 'out of good manners'.

1212. *auctours shal I finden* 'writers are to be found who have expressed this opinion'.

1214. *than drede you noght to been a cokewold* 'then you needn't fear being made a cuckold'.

1215. *also moot I thee* 'as I hope to prosper'.

1216. *grete wardeyns upon chastitee* 'wonderful guardians of chastity'.

1217. *I knowe youre delit* 'I recognize your need for sexual pleasure'.

1218. *fulfille youre worldly appetit* 'satisfy your sexual urge'.

1224–5. *take youre aventure of the repair that shal be to youre hous*
'take your chance of what may follow the stream of visitors
whom I shall attract to your house': i.e. my infidelity.

1226. *may wel be* 'very likely'.

1227. *yourselven* 'for yourself'; *selven* being inflected as in line
1155 above.

   wheither that yow liketh 'whichever pleases you'.

1228. *aviseth him* 'takes counsel with himself', 'reflects'.

1233. *and moost honour* 'and bring most dignity and respect'.

1234. *I do no fors* 'it's of no consequence to me'.

1236. *gete of yow maistrie* 'gained the upper hand over you'.

1237. *as me lest* 'as it suits me'.

1242. *I moote sterven wood* 'I may die insane'.

1243. *but I to yow be also good and trewe* 'if I am not both
virtuous and faithful to you'.

1245. *and but I be to-morn* 'and if tomorrow I am not':
referring to the day that is about to break.

   to seene 'to see': an example of the inflected infinitive.

1248. *my lyf and deth* 'my existence'.

1249. *cast up the curtin* 'lift up the curtain' surrounding a
four-poster bed. Similarly in *Gawayn and the Green Knight*,
1185, when the hero hears the lady in his bedchamber, 'a
corner of the cortin he cast up a littel'.

1253. *his herte bathed in a bath of blisse* 'almost out of his mind
with joy'.

1256. *doon him plesance or liking* 'give him pleasure or enjoyment'.

1259. *fressh abedde* 'full of sexual vigour'.

1260. *grace t'overbide* 'power, or luck, to outlive'.

1263. *nigardes of dispence* 'misers'.

APPENDIX 1

CHAUCER'S
'BALLADE OF GENTILLESSE'

GENTILLESSE

Moral Balade of Chaucier

The firste stok, fader of gentilesse—
What man that claimeth gentil for to be
Must folowe his trace, and alle his wittes dresse
Vertu to sewe, and vices for to flee.
5   For unto vertu longeth dignitee,
And noght the revers, saufly dar I deme,
Al were he mitre, croune, or diademe.

This firste stok was ful of rightwisnesse,
Trewe of his word, sobre, pitous, and free,
10   Clene of his gost, and loved besinesse,
Ayeinst the vice of slouthe, in honestee;
And, but his heir love vertu, as dide he,
He is noght gentil, thogh he riche seme,
Al were he mitre, croune, or diademe.

15   Vice may wel be heir to old richesse;
But ther may no man, as men may wel see,
Bequethe his heir his vertuous noblesse:
That is appropred unto no degree
But to the firste fader in magestee,
20   That maketh hem his heires that him queme,
Al were he mitre, croune, or diademe.

NOTES TO APPENDIX 1

1. *stok* 'progenitor of a family or race'. It is uncertain whether Chaucer means Adam, the father of mankind, or God, 'the fader of gentillesse' from whom men must derive their virtuous quality: see *The Wife of Bath's Tale*, 1162, where following Dante he makes the Lady remark that 'gentillesse cometh fro God allone', and lines 8–9 and 19 below.

3. *folowe his trace* 'follow his footsteps', imitate him.

3–4. *alle his wittes dresse vertu to sewe* 'direct his whole endeavour towards virtuous behaviour'.

5. *longeth* 'belongs'.

6. *saufly dar I deme* 'I may confidently affirm'.

7. *al were he mitre, croune, or diademe* 'whether he happen to wear mitre, crown or diadem'; as bishop, king or emperor.

8. *this firste stok was* The tense of the verb suggests that Chaucer is not referring to God, whose virtue is undiminished, but to man's uncorrupted nature before the Fall; possibly drawing additional ideas from the mythology of the Golden Age.

 rightwisnesse 'righteousness'.

9. *pitous, and fre* 'compassionate and generous'. Deep feeling for the distress of others, and liberality in giving—of whatever kind—are two of the associated qualities of gentillesse. The 'nigardes of dispence' whom the Wife curses at the end of her Tale are villeins by nature, whatever their social status.

10. *clene of his gost* 'pure in spirit'.

11. *in honestee* 'decently, in a manner befitting his position'. The modern sense of the term dates from the late sixteenth century.

12. *but* 'unless', 'except'.

15. *vice may wel be heir to old richesse* 'it may well happen that the inheritor of a wealthy estate is morally degenerate'. Cf. *The Wife of Bath's Tale*, 1151: 'a lordes sone [may] do shame and vileynie'. The phrase 'old richesse', which also appears in *The Wife of Bath's Tale*, 1110 and 1118, is probably Chaucer's rendering of 'antica richezza' in Dante's *Convivio*.

16–17. *ther may no man...bequethe his heir his vertuous noblesse*
Cf. *The Wife of Bath's Tale*, 1121–2:

> Yet may they nat biquethe, for no thing,
> To noon of us hir vertuous living.

18. *appropred unto no degree* 'assigned exclusively to no particular social class'.

19. *the first fader in magestee* Here Chaucer alludes unambiguously to God. The reference makes it seem likely that God, and not Adam, is meant in the opening lines of stanzas 1 and 2.

20. *that him queme* 'who please him', by their virtuous living.

APPENDIX 2

THEOPHRASTUS ON MARRIAGE

The passage which follows represents the views of 'Theofraste', whom the Wife mentions at line 671, upon the married state. Theophrastus, the friend to whom Aristotle bequeathed his library, was himself a philosopher; but this attributed work is known only through St Jerome, who quotes from it approvingly in the course of his treatise against Jovinian. The long quotation provided Chaucer with material which he incorporates into *The Wife's Prologue*, lines 235–315, where the Wife is made to repeat the substance of Theophrastus's satirical account of wifely behaviour in the form of a spirited attack upon exasperating husbands. The passage is included here for its obvious importance as source-material, but also as a demonstration of the scholarly interests which underlie and impel Chaucer's writing, even when—as here—he seems to be drawing exclusively upon his own close observation of human life. Numbers inside brackets refer to parallel passages of *The Wife's Prologue*. The translation is that of W. H. Fremantle, *The Principal Works of St Jerome* (Oxford, 1893).

A wise man, therefore, must not take a wife. For in the first place his study of philosophy will be hindered, and it is impossible for anyone to attend to his books and to his wife. Wives want many things—costly dresses, gold, jewels, great outlay, maid-servants, all kinds of furniture, litters and gilded coaches. Then come curtain-lectures[1] the livelong night: she complains that one lady goes out better-dressed than she; that another is looked up to by all. 'I am a poor despised nobody at the ladies' assemblies.' 'Why did you ogle that creature next door?' 'Why were you talking to the maid?' 'What did you bring from the market?' 'I am not allowed to have a single friend or companion' [236–45]. There may be in some neighbouring city the wisest of teachers; but if we have a wife we can neither leave her behind nor take the burden with us. To support a poor wife is hard; to put up with a rich one is torture [248–52]. Notice, too, that in the case of a wife you cannot pick or choose; you must take her as you find her. If she has a bad temper, or is a fool, if she has a blemish, or is proud, or has bad breath, whatever her fault may be—all this we learn after marriage. Horses, asses, cattle, even slaves of the smallest worth, clothes, kettles, wooden seats, cups and earthenware pitchers, are first tried and then bought: a wife is the only thing that is not shown before she is married, for fear she may not give satisfaction [285–92].

Our gaze must always be directed to her face, and we must always praise her beauty: if you look at another woman, she thinks that she is out of favour. She must be called 'my lady', her birthday must be kept, we must swear by her health and wish that she may survive us. Respect must be paid to the nurse, to the nursemaid, to the father's slave [293–301]; to the foster-child, to the handsome hanger-on, to the curled darling who manages her affairs [303–5], and to the eunuch who ministers to the safe indulgence of her lust; names which are only a cloak for adultery. Upon whomsoever she sets her heart, they must have her love, though they want her not. If you give her the management of the whole house, you must yourself be her slave. If you reserve something for yourself, she will think you are not loyal to her [308–11]; but she will turn to strife and hatred, and unless you quickly take care, she will have the poison ready. . . .

But what is the good of even a careful guardian, when an

---

[1] '*curtain-lecture*: a reproof given by a wife to her husband in bed' (Johnson).

unchaste wife cannot be watched [357–61], and a chaste one ought not to be? For necessity is but a faithless keeper of chastity, and she alone really deserves to be called chaste who is free to sin if she chooses [322]. If a woman be fair, she soon finds lovers; if she be ugly, it is easy to be wanton. It is difficult to guard what many desire. It is annoying to have what no one thinks worth possessing [253–6; 271–2]. But the misery of having an ugly wife is less than that of keeping watch on a beautiful one. Nothing is safe for which a whole population sighs and longs. One man entices with his figure, another with his brains, another with his wit, another with his liberality [257–61]. Somehow or other the fortress is captured which is attacked on all sides [263–4]. Men marry, indeed, in order to get a housekeeper, to solace weariness, and to banish solitude; but a faithful slave is a far better manager, more submissive to the master, more observant of his ways, than a wife who thinks she proves herself mistress if she acts in opposition to her husband— that is, if she does what pleases her, not what she is bidden.

GLOSSARY

abedde in bed
abide wait, remain, stay;
 (l. 979) endure, sustain
abroche broach, pierce
a-caterwauled caterwauling,
 behaving lasciviously
accordinge agreeing
acorded reconciled, agreed
adoun down
again (l. 675) against; (l. 1000)
 towards
agast terrified
agilte guilty
agoon ago
agrief ill, unkindly
al although; everything
al and som the whole matter

alenge miserable
algate continually
algates always, in every way
allies kindred, relatives
allone (l. 444) exclusively;
 (l. 885) alone
al so just as
alway, alwey always,
 continually
amended corrected, improved
amendere improver
a-morwe next day
and if if, if but
angre anger
a-night at night
annexed attached, joined to

Glossary

anon immediately after, straightway

answeren answer

apert plain, straightforward

apparaille dress

appetit sexual desire

a-rewe in succession

array (l. 235) order, arrangement, state; (l. 289) dress, attire; (l. 1075) preparations

arriven reach, come to

artow are you

as as if

ascendent see note, l. 613

assailled assaulted, attacked

assay test

assayed tested, tried

asterte escape

astrologien astrologer

atte at the

attendance dutiful service, attentiveness

auctoritee authority

auctour author

auncestre ancestor

avante, avaunte boast

aventure chance, luck

Averill April

aviseth reflects, considers

a-werke to work

axe ask

ay always

ba kiss, (as a child)

bacin basin

bad commanded

bakward backwards

bar bore, possessed

bareyne barren, infertile

barly-breed barley bread

be war take care

been be, are

beere bier

benedicite! God bless us!

ber bear

berd beard

bere behave

bere on honde delude, mislead

bernes barns

best animal

bet better

bete beaten

bicam suited

bifel happened

biforn in front

bigon provided, established

bigonne started

biheste promise

bileeve believe

biquethe bequeath

biraft(e) deprived of

biseke implore

bishrewe curse

bisie busy

bisinesse (l. 933) attentive service; (l. 1196) industriousness, hard work

bistowe spend

bithinke imagine

bitokeneth signifies, denotes

bitore bittern

bitterly painfully

bitwix between

biwreyed revealed, confessed

blisful happy

blisse joy

blissed blessed

blive quickly, forthwith

bobance boast

bode bidden, commanded

boghte bought, redeemed

bombleth booms

bon bone

bonde bound

boote good
bord table
borel coarse woollen clothes
boren born
bounden bound
bountee virtue, excellence
bour bed-chamber, inner room
bowen give way
breed bread
bren bran
brenne burn
brenneth burns
brent burnt
breste burst, break
breyde awoke, started
bridel bridle, management
bringere-out encourager
brinne burn
burghes boroughs, towns
but (l. 214) unless, except;
  (l. 784) if; (l. 1079) only
but if unless
by in respect of
bye buy
cacche catch, take
calle head-dress
cam returned
care worry
cas (l. 165) affair; (l. 665)
  respect, manner of means
cast throw, lift
certeinly in truth
certes assuredly
certeyn assuredly
chaast chaste
chaffare trading, business
chalenge claim
chamberere chambermaid
chambre room
charge moral weight,
  importance
charitee charitable works

cheep bargain
cheere appearance, behaviour
chees choose
chepe trade, bargain
cherl churl, coarse person
chese choose, decide
cheste coffin
chidde scolded, reproached
chide nag
chiertee affection, fondness
chiste chest, coffer
clamour outcry
clawe rub, scratch
clene (l. 598) trim, shapely;
  (l. 944) undefiled
clepe call
cleped called
clerk scholar, learned man
clooth garment
clothes material
cokewold cuckold
colour excuse, pretence
comanden command
compaignye company
comth comes
conclusion purpose
conseil secret, intention
conseille advise
conseilling advising
constellacioun combination of
  heavenly bodies and
  influences
constreyned compelled
continueel continual, endless
contraried opposed, disputed
contrarious self-willed, perverse
contrarius contrary, unlike
coost coast, country
corps dead body
costage cost, expense
coveiteth (l. 266) desires
  sexually; (l. 1187) covets

coverchief head-covering
cow chough
crave yearn, beg
crispe curly
Crist Christ
Cristen Christian
croce cross
cure heed, attention
curius skilfully made,
  elaborate
curtin curtain
custume habit
daliaunce flirtation
dampnacioun damnation
dampned condemned
dart form of prize
daun sir, lord
daunce dance
daunger power, control
daungerous disdainful,
  grudging, hard to please
daunted intimidated
dawed dawned
debaat argument
dede act
dedis acts
deed dead
deef deaf
deel bit
deere expensive
defenced forbade
degree (l. 404) way, fashion;
  (l. 626) social rank or status
delit pleasure, often sexual
derkeste darkest
desiren desire
desolat powerless
despit anger
despitus cruel
desport amusement
dettour debtor
devise imagine

devine guess
devocioun devotion
deyde died
deye die
deyntee value, pleasure
dide did
diffinicioun restriction,
  limitation
dighte lie with, lay with
diligence heedfulness,
  endeavour to please
discrecioun prudence,
  discretion
disfigure deformity
dishonour disgrace, shame
disparaged dishonoured
dispence liberal spending,
  extravagance
displeseth annoys, offends
disport amusement, pleasure
disposicioun nature,
  constitution of planet or sign
diverse different
doon do, done
dorste dared
dostow do you
dotage second childhood,
  folly
dotard imbecile, old fool
doute doubt
doutelees without doubt
draughte measure of drink
drede doubt, question
dronke(n) drunk
dronkenesse drunken state
dropping dripping, leaking
drow drew, approached
duc duke
dwelle remain
dyde would die
ech a side every side
eek also, as well

eelde old age

eftsoones immediately following

elde old age

eldres ancestors

elles else

emperice empress

empoisoned poisoned

enchanted bewitched

enforce strengthen

engendreth produces

engendrure procreation

enquere ask questions

ensample example

entendeth endeavours, aims

entente intention

entremette interfere, meddle

envenime poison, corrupt

envie envy

er before

er that before

ere ear

erl earl

erthe earth

ese delight, pleasure

esed pleased, satisfied

est east

estaat social rank, condition

eterne on live immortal

even evening

evere in oon continually

everemo constantly

evere yet always

everich everyone

every deel every bit, completely

exaltacioun planetary position of greatest influence

exaltat exalted, in great power

excepcion objection

expert experienced, skilled

expres (l. 27) clearly; (l. 61) definite, explicit; (ll. 719, 1169) explicitly stated

eyleth ails

fader father

fadres father's

faierye fairy-folk

faille fail, fall short

fair pleasant, beautiful

faire (l. 222) courteously, kindly; (l. 1142) well

fairnesse beauty, good looks

fals false, deceptive

falwes fallow ground

fantasie (l. 190) inclination; (l. 516) capricious desire, whim

fare get on

fareth behaves

fast (l. 283) secure, caught; (l. 672) eagerly

faste (l. 652) strictly; (l. 970) near

fawe willing, glad

fee possessions, money

feelinge emotional character

feend fiend, devil

feeste feast

felawe companion, close friend

fer far

ferforth far

ferthe fourth

fest fist

fet fetched, brought

fey faith

feyned feigned, assumed

fil(le) fell

filthe dirtiness

fine finish, stop

firy fiery

fit exciting time
fle run away
fo enemy
folwed followed
fonde try, endeavour
foore path, footsteps
for that because, since
forbede deny
forbedeth forbids
forbere endure, submit to
forgat forgot
forgo give up, lose
fors importance, consequence
forthermo in addition, moreover
foryeve forgive
foul(e) (l. 265) ugly, unattractive; (l. 460) wicked; (l. 485) improper, immoral; (l. 963) disgraceful; (l. 1069) shamefully
fouler uglier
freendes friends
freletee frailty, weakness of the flesh
frely liberally, generously
frere friar
frete devour, consume
fro from
ful very
fulfild filled full
fulfille satisfy
fully completely, entirely
fyn fine, pure
gale cry out, exclaim
galle sore spot
galwes gallows
gan did
gat-tothed widely spaced teeth
geestes tales, romances
generacioun reproduction

generally as a general principle
genterie nobility
gentil noble, gentle of birth and character
gentillesse delicacy, good breeding, nobility
gentils gentlemen
gentrie high birth
gesse suppose, judge
gete(n) obtained
gilt guilt, sin
giltelees guiltless, undeserved
gites gowns, dresses
glade happy
gladly eagerly
glose (l. 119) interpret, explain; (l. 509) cajole, persuade
glosen supply commentary
good (l. 231) advantage, profit; (l. 310) goods, property
goost (l. 273) goes; (l. 986) spirit
gossib intimate friend
governance control, rule
grace (l. 553) credit, honour; (l. 746) fortune; (l. 895) favour, mercy
grave buried
grece grease, fat
greet great
greve grieve, vex
grint grinds
grisly terrible, dreadful
grucche grumble, complain
grucching grumbling
habitacioun dwelling
hadden had
half, a Goddes in God's name
halles halls
halt holds, considers

Glossary

halwes shrines
han have
happed befell, occurred
hardinesse boldness
harneys equipment, sexual organs
hastow have you
haukes hawks
have (l. 530) keep
hawe hawthorn-berry
heed head
heer hair
heere hear, listen to
heeste behest, bidding
heigh high, noble
helde holde
hele conceal
helpeth assists, profits
hem them, themselves
hende handy, pleasant, courteous
hente seized, embraced
herbes herbs
heres hair
herkne listen
herkneth listen
herte heart
hevynesse depression, sadness
hidestow do you hide
hight promised
highte was called
him himself
hir their
hire (l. 533) her; (l. 1008) reward, payment
holde (l. 135) obliged; (l. 198) keep, observe; (l. 523) considered, judged
holden considered
holour lecher, adulterer
hond hand
honour high respect, reverence
hool whole, sound

hoolly wholly, entirely
hooly holy
hoom home
hoot hot
hors horses
hoten be called
hou how
housbondrie household goods
hye high
hyeste highest, best
ilke same
impossible impossibility
in (l. 350) dwelling; (l. 796) on
in honde in hand, in his control
inclinacioun impulse
incubus evil spirit
Inde the Indes, India
in-feere together
iren iron; the axe
ivel evil
jalousie jealousy
jangleresse chatterbox
jape trick
jolitee gaiety, sexual liveliness
joly merry, lively
jolynesse cheerfulness, amorousness, joie de vivre
juggement judgement, wise choice
justise judge
kan know, know how, understand
kaynard dotard, old fool
keep care, heed
kep regard, notice
kepe (l. 263) keep, preserve, defend; (l. 710) be constant to, preserve
kept saved, preserved
kichenes kitchens
kike kick

kinde (l. 1101) stock; (l. 1149) nature

kindely naturally, as a characteristic

kitte cut

knave (l. 253) crafty rogue; (l. 1190) servant, menial

knowen discover, learn

koude could, knew how

lasse less

lat let

lat be give over, drop

lavour basin

lawe custom, fashion

lecchour lecher, profligate

leef page

leere learn

leeste, atte at the least

leeve dear

lemman mistress, concubine

lenger longer

leon lion

leonesse lioness

lest please, wish

lete (l. 31) forsake; (l. 767) let, allowed

lette be hindered

lettest hinder

leve (l. 319) permit; (l. 908) permission, leave

leveful permissible

levene lightning-flash

levere rather

leyser leisure, opportunity

licence permission

lie blaze

lief beloved

lige liege, sovereign

lightly easily, quickly

liked attracted

likerous lustful

likerousnesse sexual eagerness

liking (l. 736) sensuality; (l. 1256) pleasure, enjoyment

likne liken, compare

limitacioun limit, appointed district

limitour limiter; friar with an allotted district

linage lineage, family

line family descent

list(e) (l. 633) wish, desire; (l. 634) ear

litel small

lith lies

live life

lives biographies

loke lock

lond (l. 204) land; (l. 867) country

looke who whoever

loore teaching, instruction

loothly loathsome, repulsive

lordinges gentlemen

lorel wretch

lough (l. 672) laughed; (l. 1101) low, base

love lover

lowe wretched

lust (l. 78) wishes; (l. 416) sexual appetite; (l. 736) lust, immoderate desire

lusty pleasant, vigorous, exuberant

lyen lie

made composed, wrote

maden made, caused

magestee majesty

maide virgin

maidenhed virginity

maister lord

maistow you may

maistrie superior force, victory

make mate, spouse
malencolie melancholy, ill-temper, sullenness
maner(e) kind of
manere (l. 839) fashion, manner
many on many a one
Marcien Martialist
mareys marsh
Martes Mars's
mateere matter, affair
matere (l. 516) business, subject
matins morning prayers
maugree despite
me myself
mede meadow
meene mean
mekely meek
meschance misfortune
meschief mishap, injury
mette dreamt
might power, ability
mighte could
mire bog, swamp
mirie cheerful, gay
mirily happily, joyously; (l. 1192) jokingly
mirthe joke, laugh
misavise act ill-advisedly
mite parasitic insect
mo more
mooder mother
moore and lesse completely, as a whole
mooste (l. 505) most; (l. 1041) dearest, greatest
moot may, must
mooten must
mordred murdered
morne grieve
morwe morning

morweninges mornings
most(e) must
motthes moths
muchel much, far
murmur grumbling, complaint
myn mine, my
nacioun birth
nam am not
namely especially
namo no other
namoore no more
nath has not
nathelees none the less
natureel natural
natureelly naturally, by nature
ne not, nor
nece niece, female relative
necligence negligence, carelessness
nedely of necessity
nekke-boon neckbone, neck
nel will not
nice foolish, ignorant
nicetee lust
nigard miser
nil will not
nis is not
niste knew not
noblesse nobility, high rank
n'of nor of
noght not, not at all
nolde would not, do not wish, refuse to
none no
nones occasion, purpose
noon no, none
norice nurse
ny near, close
o one
octogamie marrying eight times

of off
office (l. 127) physical
  function; (l. 1137) duty,
  service
on a day one day
on honde engaged upon
ones once
onis once
oon one
oore ore
oother other person
open-heveded bare-headed
operacioun action,
  performance
opinion belief
oppressioun violation, rape
oratories small rooms within a
  monastery
otheres the other's
ouche clasp
out of doute for a certainty
oute set out, expose for sale
outher either
outrely utterly, completely
over al everywhere
owene own
pace pass, leave
paid satisfied, content
parage birth, rank
paramour mistress
paraventure perhaps
pardee par dieu; by God
parfit perfect
pees be quiet
perree precious stones
persevere continue
persone person, actual self
pestilence plague
peyne trouble, distress, grief
peyntede painted
pie magpie
pine agony

pistel message
pith vigour
pitously piteously
plante slip, cutting
plesance pleasure
pleye (l. 192) play, entertain,
  sport; (l. 245) make an
  outing
pleyes of miracles miracle-plays
pleyne complain
plight (l. 790) plucked;
  (l. 1009) pledge
poure gaze
poverte poverty
povre poor
praktike mode of action, habit
preambulacioun preambling,
  making a prologue
preche lecture
prechestow you lecture
preching sermons
prechour preacher
precious fine, costly
precius fastidious,
  over-refined
preciously in an expensive
  manner
preef, with ivel bad luck to
  you!
prees crowd, throng
preesse press, beset, assail
preferre take precedence over
prente imprint
preye beg
preyeden prayed, besought
preyse praise
preysed commended
priketh spurs
pris esteem, regard
privee (l. 620) private,
  intimate; (l. 1114)
  withdrawn, unassuming

Glossary

prively furtively, secretly
privetee secret personal affairs
propre one's own
proprely (l. 224) properly, exactly; (l. 1191) intrinsically, of itself
prowesse excellence, moral goodness
prys worth
pured refined
purgacioun excretion
purpos object, intention
pursute petition, entreaty
purveiance foresight, provision for the future
purveye provide
purveyed provided
queynte (sb.) woman's sexual parts; (adj.) curious, odd
quit(e) repaid
quitte repaid
quod said
quoniam thingummebob
radde read
rafte took away, robbed
ragerie wantonness, passion
rake-stele rake-handle
raunson ransom, payment
recche heed, care
red read
redde read
redeth discover the meaning of
redresse amend, put right
reed red
reedeth read, study
refreshed (l. 38) reinvigorated, relieved; (l. 146) provided food
rekketh concerns, troubles
remembreth comes to mind
remenant remainder, rest
renne run

renneth runs
renomee renown
rente tore
repair resort, habitual visiting
repreeve reprove, reproach
repreve reproach
requere demand
resonable rational, sensible
revelour riotous person
rewe, by one after another
reyn rain
reysed raised
richesse wealth
right exactly, just
right naught not at all
right tho right then, immediately
riot wanton or extravagant behaviour
Romain Roman
roode beem rood-beam; see note l. 496
roos rose
roule gad about
rowne whisper
rubriche rubric, religious directive
rude poor, humble, rough
salwes willow-branches
sapience wisdom
souf safe
saufly safely
saugh saw
savacioun salvation
save except
savoure taste, smell
sawe saying
say saw
sayde ventured, put to the test
science learning
scole university school
seche seek

134

Glossary

secree discreet

seel seal

seist sayest, say

seistow you say

seke seek, search for

selde rarely, seldom

sely (l. 132) simple, blessed; (l. 370) harmless, innocent

senge singe

sentence opinion, pronouncement

sepulcre tomb

serchen visit, haunt

seten sat

sette reckoned, counted

seyden said

seydest said

seye (l. 53) say, speak; (l. 59) see; (l. 552) seen

seye nay deny

seyn say

shame modesty

shap sexual parts

shapen (l. 139) fashioned, formed; (l. 554) intended

shende destroy

sheres scissors

sherte shirt

shette shut

shewe reveal, disclose

shifte to provide, distribute

shipnes stables, sheds

sho shoe

shorte shorten

shrewe (sb.) wicked person, scoundrel; (vb.) beshrew, curse

shrewed wicked

shrewednesse wickednesse

shul (l. 181) ought; (l. 332) shall; (l. 343) must

side body

sik illness

siker sure, certain

siketh sighs

singeth sings

sire head of the house

sith since

sleighte craft, cunning

slik sleek, smooth

smal little

smale slender

smok smock, undergarment

smoot struck

sodeynly suddenly

soffre put up with, endure

sojourne delay, tarry

solempnitee ceremoniousness, pomp

som time once, at one time

someres summer

somme some

somonour summoner

sondry various

song sang

songen sang

sonne-beem sunbeam

soore sorely, painfully

sooth truly, truth

sorwe sorrow, grief

sorwe, with devil take you!

sory sorrowful, sad

sothe (l. 46) truly; (l. 931) truth

soun sound

soutiltee subtlety, artifice

soverainetee supremacy

spak spoke

spareth refrain, desist

spaynel spaniel

specially in particular

spectacle eye-glass

spek speak, say

spekestow do you say

spille put to death, kill

Glossary

spilt ruined, lost

spitously spitefully, maliciously

spyen spy upon, watch

squiereth escorts, accompanies

stable constant, faithful

statut statute, law

sterte leap, run

sterven die

stibourn stubborn

stifly boldly

stille silent

stirte started, leapt

stonde stand, affirm

stoundes times, seasons

strange external, adventitious

subtilly (l. 499) subtly, with great craftsmanship; (l. 956) carefully, cleverly

suffisant satisfactory, adequate

suffiseth contents, satisfies

suffrable patient, long-suffering

suffre allow, grant

suffreth suffer, endure, be patient

suppose conceive, guess

suretee security

suspecioun suspicion

suster sister

swal swelled

swere swear false oaths

swich such

swinke labour, toil

swogh swoon

swoor swore

taak take

taak keep observe

taken accepted, received

talis tales, gossip

Taur Taurus, the Bull; second sign of the Zodiac

teche instruct, tell

temporel temporal; worldly, impermanent

terme duration

t'espie to spy upon

testament will

thanne then

thar needs it

that who

thee prosper

thenketh think, consider (imp.)

thenne thence

ther wherever

ther as where

therafter after it

therbifoore previously

therby by it, to it

therto in addition

therwithal in addition

thikke thick, numerous

thilke that same

thing something

thise these

tho (l. 195) those; (l. 721) then

thogh though

thonder thunder

thonder-dint thunderclap

thoughte seemed

thow thou

thral slave

thrifty respectable, fit to be seen

thropes thorpes, villages

thurgh through

tikled gave pleasure to

tikleth gratifies, excites

tobroke broken

tolde reckoned, accounted

to-morn tomorrow

tomorwe tomorrow

tonge tongue

tonne tun, barrel

took struck
toold disclosed
tormentrie torture, agony
touche have intercourse with
toures towers
tourne turn
t'overbide to outlive
to-yeere this year
tree wood
treson betrayal
tresoor wealth
trewely truly
tribulacioun misery,
  oppression
trouthe troth
trowe believe, think
trusteth believe, depend
twelf-month year
tweye two
twiste wrung, tormented
undermeles afternoons
undertake declare, warrant
unnethe(s) scarcely, hardly at
  all
unright injury, wrong
up and down in every respect
upon on my person
upright supine, at full length
us selven ourselves
usage custom
usinge wont, habituated
vacacioun freedom, rest from
  work
Venerien influenced by Venus
verraily truly
verray veritable, genuine,
  absolute
vertu virtue, power
vice defect, deformity
vigilies vigils; religious
  services held on eves of
  feast days

vileynie (l. 34) reproach,
  wrong; (l. 962) shameful
  deed
vileyns villainous
vinolent tipsy, full of wine
visage face
visitacioun trip, excursion
vois voice
waite what whatever
walweth tosses
warde-cors bodyguard
wardeyn keeper, defender
ware wares, merchandise
wast needless expense
wax became
wedde marry
wedding marrying
weel well
weilawey alas!
weive refrain from, forsake
welde manage, control
welked withered
wench common woman,
  mistress
wende go, depart
wene suppose, imagine
wenestow do you suppose
wered wore
wereth wears
werne refuse, forbid
werre war, strife
wexe wax, increase
whan when
what why
wheither (l. 898) whether;
  (l. 1227) whichever
wher where
which that whom
whine whinny
widwe widow
wight person
wilde violent, destructive

wilful willing, voluntary
winde turn, roll about
winne (l. 414) get profit;
  (l. 961) gain
winning profit, gain
wirche act, perform
wirking influence
wisdam wisdom
wise fashion, manner
wiste knew
wit reason
wite blame, reproach
withal as well, also
witing knowledge
wo grief, misery
wode wood
wol(e) (l. 209) will; (l. 307)
  wish, desire
wolde wished to
woldest would like to
wolt wilt, will
woltow would you
wont was accustomed
wood mad, furious
woot (l. 27) know; (l. 124)
  discovers, proves
worldly professional
wormes maggots, grubs
wostow do you know
wreke avenged
writ writes
wroghte made, created
wrong wrung, pinched

wroot wrote
wrothe angry
wy why
wyf wife; woman of humble
  rank or employment
wyfhod wifehood, married
  state of a woman
wys manner
yaf gave
ybroght brought
ydo done, finished
yelden yield up, surrender
yen eyes
yeve give
yeve up surrender
yeven given
yerne eagerly, quickly
yflatered flattered
ygrave buried
yif give
yifte gift
yit yet
yive given
ylimed caught, as with
  bird-lime
ynogh enough
yowthe youth
yplesed pleased
yrekened reckoned, considered
ysowe sowed
ystint at an end
ywis certainly, truly
ywroght created